No Controlling Legal Authority:
Essays on the Insignificant Legal Issues of Our Times

By Bill Haltom

FOR JACK GREEN, WITH WARM REGARDS!

Bill Haltom

TBAPress

No Controlling Legal Authority:
Essays on the Insignificant Legal Issues of Our Times

TBAPress

Published by the Tennessee Bar Association Press.
Book design by Landry Butler
Illustrations by Dave Jendras

Additional copies of this book may be ordered
from the publisher at
https://www.tba.org/TennBarU/bookstore.html
or by calling 1-800-899-6993.
$15. Add $5 for postage and handling.

ISBN: 0-9701286-1-4

Many of these works are reprinted from *The Tennessee Bar Journal*, *The Commercial Appeal* and *The Brunswick News*, with permission.

Illustrations by David Jendras

Front cover: No Controlling Legal Authority

Part 1: Of Mice and Men: *Mickey v. the Ghost of Sonny Bono*

Part 2: The Feminization of the Profession,
or How to Handle a Speeding Ticket in Arkansas

Part 3: Andy of Mayberry, Esquire

Part 4: Where Will Clark Kent Change his Clothes?

Part 5: The Geeking of the Profession

Part 6: The Only Acceptable Apology is a Rectangular One

Part 7: Atticus

"My lawyer tells me there is no controlling legal authority."

—Vice President Al Gore, 1996,
in an early endorsement of this book

> **"Anyone who takes himself too seriously always runs the risk of looking ridiculous; anyone who can consistently laugh at himself does not."** —Vaclav Havel

Lawyers have excellent senses of humor — after all, what other profession can claim such an embarrassment of riches when it comes to jokes?

In truth, it takes a particularly keen sense of comedy, as well as a keen legal wit, to mine the humor from the serious work of the law. My friend Bill Haltom has both the comedic and lawyerly sensibility to pull off this considerable task. The humor collected in *No Controlling Legal Authority: Essays on the Insignificant Legal Issues of Our Times* reveals a subtle and wry wit that is a treat to read.

My friendship with Bill spans nearly 25 years, since our days in the American Bar Association Young Lawyers Division. Back then, we were young bucks. Nowadays, we're (hopefully) closer to elder statesmen, and in the intervening years we've had in common those experiences that move you from being an inexperienced lawyer to a more experienced one. The long nights and the pressure so peculiar to our profession can be a burden or a boon, and the form these challenges take on more often than not is determined by one's ability to find the humor in a given situation. Hopefully we can all laugh at life's absurdities. But on those occasions when the humor simply escapes you, pick up *No Controlling Legal Authority*. Not only is it an excellent source of laughter, guaranteed to ease the stress of practicing law, but all of the proceeds go to benefit the Tennessee Legal Community Foundation, a not-for-profit organization dedicated to furthering the ideals of professionalism in the practice of law and to providing education about and access to the legal system.

Laughter: it's not only good for your soul — now, it also benefits the legal profession.

—Robert J. Grey Jr., President, American Bar Association

Author's Note

I'm blessed to share a life with two fascinating groups of people — lawyers and journalists. For 27 years I have been a trial lawyer with a great firm. My colleagues at Thomason Hendrix are my partners in the truest and best sense of the word.

I'm also a bar junkie. My closest friends are my fellow lawyers in the Tennessee Bar Association. We work together, vacation together, party together, and — above all — attend Tennessee Vol football games together. I am particularly indebted to Charles Swanson, Pam Reeves and Allan Ramsaur for sticking with me when I've ridden tall in the saddle and also when I've been thrown off my horse.

And I'm a Walter Mitty journalist who has been fortunate to have some wonderful editors who make me look like I know what I'm doing. These include Suzanne Robertson of the *Tennessee Bar Journal*, Dan Kim of the ABA *Journal*, Gary Hengstler of The National Center for the Courts and Media, Howard Vogel of TBA*Link*, Leanne Kleinmann and Emily Adams Keplinger of *The Memphis Commercial Appeal*, and Kerry Klumpe of *The Brunswick News*. Special thanks go to Landry Butler of the TBA Press whose design skills transformed my crazy columns into the epic literary masterpiece you now hold in your hands, bless you.

And above all, I'm blessed to share a life with one very special lawyer, Claudia Swafford Haltom. She is the love of my life for many reasons, not the least of which is that she always laughs at my jokes.

Finally, this book is dedicated to the memory of the late John Hester, my high school English teacher, debate coach and speech teacher. Mr. Hester inspired me to become a lawyer and a writer. Next to my father, he is the finest man I have ever known.

—Bill Haltom

Contents

Part V: Geeks, Gadgets and Gizmos
(Not to be Confused With the Law Firm by the Same Name)

Part VI: Litigation Means Never Having to Say You're Sorry

Part VII: But Seriously, Folks

PART I:
TRIALS AND ERRORS

ABC's Monday Night Jury Trial:
Are You Ready for Some Lawsuits?

Ever since the O.J. trial, litigation has threatened to replace baseball as our official national pastime.

During most of the decade of the '90s, every time I turned on my television, I was forced to watch news broadcasts concerning the O. J. Simpson legal proceedings. Twenty-four hours a day, seven days a week, we were treated to non-stop coverage of the *State of California v. O. J.*, starring the late Johnnie Cochran, Judge Lance Ito, Marcia Clark, F. Lee Bailey, Kato Kaelin, and Jerry Mathers as "The Beaver."

And then after O.J. I came O.J. II, the civil trial. It wasn't nearly as exciting as the criminal trial, since there was absolutely no risk that O.J. would get the death penalty or even join Martha Stewart in a minimum-security federal country club. The worst thing that could happen to O.J. in the civil trial was that he might lose his Heisman Trophy, his white Bronco, and his knit cap. Moreover, in the civil trial, O.J. was represented by a dull, boring lawyer who was no Johnnie Cochran. He didn't even make an effort to make his words rhyme during closing argument. In his defense, closing argument poetry is a lot easier in a criminal trial than in a civil trial. For example, there are many words that rhyme with "acquit." But to my knowledge, there is not a single word in the English language that rhymes with "damages."

Even when the second O.J. trial was over, the television networks continued to broadcast talk shows featuring O.J.'s lawyers, and several even became hosts of their own shows, such as "Late Night with Barry Sheck" and "The F. Lee Bailey Comedy Hour."

Lawyers now have their own network, Court TV, and some local cable companies feature the "O.J. Channel" or "O.J. Span", for those TV viewers who want to watch re-plays of his trials ("O.J. Court Classics") or coverage of O.J.'s continuing pursuit of the real killers, broadcast live from some of America's finest golf courses.

Fortunately, the "O.J. Channel" is not one of the 347 channels of quality TV entertainment I get through my local cable company. But I do get ESPN, and I watch it religiously. In fact, I not only watch ESPN on Sunday, but Monday through Saturday nights as well.

And so on a recent evening, I parked myself in my recliner, took the remote control channel changer firmly in hand, and tuned in to ESPN hoping to watch an exciting sporting event such as major league baseball, arena football, or a celebrity boxing match between Hillary Rodham Clinton and Monica Lewinsky.

But when I turned on ESPN, I didn't see Sammy Sosa or Todd Helton. I didn't see Lennox Lewis or Mike Tyson or Tonya Harding. Instead, I saw Pete Rose. But he wasn't standing on a baseball diamond or even in a casino. He was in a courtroom as the defendant in a trial. Not a real trial, mind you. It was a mock trial, and the issue wasn't whether Pete might enter prison, but rather whether he would be allowed to enter baseball's Hall of Fame.

The ESPN prosecutor, Alan Dershowitz, argued that Pete should be banned for life from Cooperstown for two reasons. First, he bet on baseball. Second, he has a haircut so bad he resembles Shemp from the Three Stooges.

Pete's defense counsel argued that even if Pete liked to gamble, his accomplishments on the diamond warranted his admission to the Hall of Fame. And taking a page out of the O.J. I defense playbook, Pete's lawyer argued to the jury that the evidence that Pete had bet on major league baseball games was actually planted in the MLB Commissioner's office by Los Angeles police detective Mark Furman.

By a vote of 8–4, the jury returned a verdict in favor of Pete's admission to the Hall of Fame. The verdict was accepted by Judge Catherine Crier, host of Court TV's "Catherine Crier Live." I'm not quite sure why she was the judge. I guess Lance Ito wasn't available.

So help me, after the jury announced its verdict, Dershowitz requested that the jury be polled "for purposes of an appeal." I'm not sure exactly where you appeal an adverse verdict from an ESPN TV show. Maybe it goes to the "Nick at Nite" Supreme Court.

Well, I'm no Gerry Spence, but I think ESPN's trial of Pete Rose was a dangerous legal precedent, putting our TV legal system on a slippery slope. Why before you know it, ABC will be broadcasting the "Monday Night Jury Trial" with Al Michaels doing the play-by-play, Nina Totenberg providing the color commentary, and Hank Williams Jr. crooning, "Are you ready for some lawsuits?!"

In fact, next Thursday night, ESPN will be broadcasting the trial of Sammy Sosa, as Sammy's lawyer tries to persuade a fair and impartial Chicago jury that the infamous corked bat was planted in the Wrigley Field dugout by St. Louis Cardinals outfielder Albert Pujols.

And I'm telling you, sports fans, it won't stop there. Next will come the trial of the Pittsburgh Pirates player who clubbed the giant sausage, and after that, we'll all tune in to ESPN to watch a celebrity jury try to decide whether Mark McGwire should be banned from Cooperstown and have a Roger Maris-style asterisk permanently connected to his name. Too bad for Mark that Johnnie Cochran is no longer around. He was the only lawyer in America who could have come up with a word to rhyme with "steroids."

Well, now that ESPN is televising lawsuits, I guess I'll just have to grab the channel changer and switch over to Cartoon Network. And when I do, I sure hope I'm not forced to watch the trial of Sponge Bob.

• • •

Of Mice and Men:
Mickey v. The Ghost of Sonny Bono

The United States Supreme Court recently heard oral argument on one of the most important legal issues of our time: Will Mickey Mouse, at long last, win his freedom, or will he continue to be haunted by the ghost of Sonny Bono?

For nearly a century, Mickey has been the intellectual property of his creator, the late Walt Disney, and after Walt's death, the Walt Disney Company.

During his long tenure as intellectual property, Mickey has become the world's most famous rodent. He is the star of stage, screen and TV, and Mousely Monarch of a Magic Kingdom that extends from sea (Disneyworld) to shining sea (Disneyland). But in just two years, Mickey may finally become a free agent, no longer controlled by the Walt Disney Company. In fact, the only thing standing between Mickey and his freedom is the ghost of Sonny Bono and the nine members of the United States Supreme Court.

As you are reading this, you no doubt think I'm goofy. But there are minnie aspects to this intriguing story, and I for one am not going to duck them, Donald.

You see, as intellectual property Mickey has been under the exclusive ownership of the Disney Company for over 70 years. But Disney's copyright on Mickey is scheduled to expire in 2004, at which time the image of Mickey passes into the public domain, making the world's most famous mouse his own man.

At this point, enter the ghost of Sonny Bono. Back in 1998, before Sonny went to Rock n' Roll Heaven, he was Congressman Sonny Bono, and he introduced a bill called "the Sonny Bono Copyright Term

Extension Act," a law that retroactively extended copyright protection from 75 years to 95 years. With the help of Disney lobbyists, Sonny got the new law enacted, effectively keeping Mickey under the exclusive control of the Walt Disney Company until 2024, enabling Disney CEO Michael Eisner to sing to Mickey, "I got you, babe!"

Suffice to say that when it came to Mickey Mouse, Sonny did not feel that Walt Disney should have to Cher and Cher alike.

Well, faster than you can say Meeska-Muska-Mouseketeer, the new federal law was challenged in the case of *Eldred v. Ashcroft*, a lawsuit that seeks to invalidate the Sonny Bono Copyright Term Extension Act of 1998. The legal beat goes on, and the case is now pending before the United States Supreme Court.

And so, the same nine people who put George Dubya "Landslide" Bush in the White House in 2000, will now soon decide whether Mickey Mouse stays in the Disney Castle for 20 more years, or whether Mickey, like his buddy Pinocchio, will have no legal strings to hold him down.

Forget about Snow White and the Seven Dwarfs. Get ready for Mickey Mouse and the nine Supreme Court Justices! Hi-ho, hi-ho! It's off to judicial chambers we go!

And it's not only Mickey's freedom that's at stake in the case of *Eldred v. Ashcroft*. Bugs Bunny is also watching this case carefully as he is now the intellectual property of AOL Time Warner. But if Mickey goes free, Bugs (who reportedly filed an amicus brief with the Supreme Court) will no doubt try to follow Mickey in the near future, and the next thing you know, Roadrunner, Wile E. Coyote, Sylvester and Tweetie Bird will also seek to be free agents in the lucrative cartoon market.

Well, when you wish upon a star, it makes no difference who you are, unless you are intellectual property in prison for another 20 years thanks to the late Sonny Bono.

I for one say, "Free Mickey!" And while we're at it, let's free Minnie and Donald and Huey and Louie and Dewey!

Why do I feel so strongly? Simple. If Mickey's lawyers can break up Disney's mouse monopoly, I may soon be able to take my kids to Six Flags Over Mickey, at greatly reduced ticket prices!

• • •

The Third Lawsuit in October

've always wondered why SEC football coaches are flanked by state troopers at football games. I first noticed this coach-and-smokies phenomenon some 30 years ago when the legendary Bear Bryant was coaching at Alabama. As the Crimson Tide raced on to the field, Coach Bear would amble slowly from the locker room, wearing his red blazer and black and white checkered hat. As he prowled the sidelines, he was always accompanied by two Alabama state troopers — one to his left, the other to his right — ready to protect him from a sudden assault by an Auburn fan.

I always thought this was sort of an overreaction. Who in the world would have attacked Bear Bryant? Johnny Majors? Of course not. Why every third Saturday in October immediately after Bama beat the Vols, old Bear and his state troopers would meet Johnny Majors and his smokies at the center of the field, where Johnny would always bow gracefully, kiss the Bear's SEC championship ring, and congratulate him on his 27th consecutive victory over the Volunteers. The Bear had nothing to fear. He needed state trooper protection about as much as Santa Claus.

But the Bear is in heaven now, and Johnny Majors got fired at Tennessee some 12 years ago because he couldn't beat Alabama. Tennessee is now coached by Phillip Fulmer, who unlike the Bear and Johnny Majors, is a man who definitely needs protection, particularly when he makes a trip to Birmingham.

Back in late July, Coach Fulmer and his fellow SEC coaches were scheduled to be in Birmingham for something called "SEC media days." But the word down in Sweet Home Alabama was that Coach Fulmer not only needed a couple of Tennessee state troopers, but maybe the entire Tennessee National Guard and at least one good lawyer as well. Coach Fulmer got the word, and apparently he was pretty concerned. So concerned that on advice of counsel he cancelled his trip to Birmingham. It was probably a smart decision, as Coach Fulmer is about as welcome in Alabama these days as the Dixie Chicks would be at the Republican National Convention.

Coach Fulmer is Public Enemy No. 1 in Alabama because a few years back, he reportedly gave NCAA investigators evidence that Alabama football coaches were doing a whole lot of cheating. Bama didn't get the death penalty, but based on Coach Fulmer singing like an orange canary, the University of Alabama football program was given more jail time than Martha Stewart.

The Crimson Tide Nation was outraged, not because Bama was caught cheating, but because most Bama fans fervently believe that Coach Fulmer is one big old cheating guy himself, and that he only turned state's evidence, so to speak, to make sure he and his fellow Vol coaches didn't go to jail as well.

Bama fans got so riled up that they did something that the Bear never did. They hired lawyers and started filing lawsuits against Coach Fulmer, the University of Tennessee, and the NCAA, alleging that there had been a vast Big Orange conspiracy to do in the football program at the University of Alabama. One Crimson Tide lawyer even threatened to serve Coach Fulmer with a subpoena the next time he showed up in Birmingham or anywhere in the great State of Alabama. (As my all-time favorite actor, Wilford Brimley, said in *Absence of Malice*, "wonderful thing, suh-pee-knees.")

The Bama battle cry is no longer Roll Tide! It's File Suit! Forget about the third Saturday in October. How about the third lawsuit in October? If you can't beat 'em, sue 'em! My high school team, the Frayser High Golden Rams, had a memorable team cheer: "We may not win the game, but we're definitely gonna win the post-game fight!" In

Bama these days, Crimson Tide fans cheer, "You may have better line-backers, but our lawyers can beat your lawyers."

Well, I'm a proud graduate of the University of Tennessee where I received my bachelor of conservative arts degree in football appreciation. Therefore, as an impartial observer, I can assure all the fine people in the State of Alabama that the University of Tennessee runs an absolutely clean football program. Each member of our team is an outstanding student-ath-uh-leat (as Coach Bill Battle used to call 'em) who excels in the classroom, particularly in challenging undergraduate courses such as "Walking." Believe it or not, that's really a course in the University of Tennessee physical education department. Reportedly, it's a much tougher course than "Sitting."

Moreover, many of the outstanding student athletes at the University of Tennessee are probably headed to law school. I say this because from what I've read in the sports pages recently, many of them already have extensive experience in our criminal justice system. This was perhaps best illustrated by a not-so-funny joke that was recently told to me by a graduate of Vanderbilt, which, I have been told, is an accredited school in Nashville.

QUESTION: What do you say a University of Tennessee football player who is wearing a coat and tie?

ANSWER: Will the defendant please rise?

When I heard this joke, I immediately had a response for my Vandy buddy.

QUESTION: What is the difference between the Vanderbilt football team and the Titanic?

ANSWER: The Titanic had a good band.

Well, here's hoping the Bama fans will let bygones be bygones and someday (say in October of 2005) welcome Coach Phil back to the great State of Alabama with open arms rather than firearms and suh-pee-knees.

Finally, I hope that the Bama fans drop their lawsuits claiming that the Vols' domination of the Tide over the past ten years has been due to a conspiracy between Coach Phil, UT, the NCAA, the FBI, the CIA, and the Farm Bureau. The Volunteers and the Crimson Tide have been doing battle for 100 years now, and we don't need a class action lawsuit on behalf of Alabama fans to help us settle our differences. We can settle them like we always do ... on the football field in October. Frankly, the Bear wouldn't have it any other way.

● ● ●

Julie v. Trish: **The Nixon Girls go to Court**

P oor Dick Nixon. Eight years after his death, he is still haunted by legal problems. And here's the really bad news. This time the case is not U.S. *v. Nixon*, it's *Julie v. Tricia!*

That's right, my fellow Americans. President Nixon's two daughters, Julie Nixon Eisenhower and Tricia Nixon Cox, are headed to court for the biggest Nixon legal battle since Leon Jaworski chased their father and his taped confessions all the way to the United States Supreme Court.

And my fellow Americans, let me make this perfectly clear. This is shaping up to be the worst legal battle yet for the late President. It's a regular Nixon family feud with Julie and Trish on opposite sides of courtrooms in Florida and California as they battle over control of the Nixon Library in Yorba Linda, California.

According to a recent article in USA *Today*, the Nixon girls don't even speak to each other these days, except through their lawyers.

So how did the Nixon girls, who once saved their dad's political career by appearing on national television with their cocker spaniel, Checkers, now find themselves on opposite sides of courtrooms in Florida and California? Well, as Deep Throat once told Bob Woodward and Carl Bernstein, "Follow the money!"

Apparently the Nixon family feud is over money, specifically Uncle Bebe's money. Uncle Bebe was Daddy Nixon's old buddy, Bebe Rebozo. I'm sure you remember Bebe. He was the Miami investor who held the unofficial position of "First Pal" in the Nixon administration.

Bebe was Dick Nixon's closest friend. Dick and Bebe fished together, snapped towels with one another in the presidential locker room, and played golf together along with other presidential buddies such as Billy Graham and Bob Hope.

Dick and Bebe were inseparable. They took long walks together on the beach at San Clemente, both relaxing in their dark blue business suits and wing tips (Air Nixons).

Thanks to Bebe, Dick was "tanned, rested and ready" in '68!

In fact, Dick and Bebe were so close, Dick did not even tape their conversations.

Bebe was also Dick's closest political advisor, masterminding such brilliant Nixon moves as making Elvis a federal narcotics agent and coming up with the catchy phrase, "I am not a crook!"

When Bebe died in 1998, he left 19 million unlaundered big ones to the Nixon library. Well, faster than you could say "executive privilege," Julie and Trish got into a fight over how the money should be spent. One thing led to another, and now it's turned out to be the biggest Nixon legal brouhaha since Bob Bork fired Archibald Cox during the Saturday night massacre in October of 1973.

In January, Julie and her supporters filed suit over Uncle Bebe's money in probate courts in Florida and California, so Julie and Trish are now clashing in a coast-to-coast, two-front, loser-leave-the-library legal battle.

This could turn out to be the worst thing to happen to the Nixon family since Dick forgot to shave before his debate with Jack Kennedy in 1960. It's a sad state of legal affairs when the Nixon girls are fighting over $19 million, given the fact that their poor late mother, Pat, once had to wear a cloth coat, rather than mink.

Well, my fellow Americans, now that we don't have Dick Nixon to kick around anymore, here's hoping his daughters will quit kicking each other and settle their differences out of court. As Daddy Dick's old buddy, Spiro Agnew, would say, "It's time for Julie and Trish to quit being a couple of nattering nabobs of negativism!"

Julie and Trish should remember what happened to their father when he went to court some 30 years ago. He not only lost his case. He also lost his job.

• • •

One Crummy Lawsuit

I love Oreo cookies. I don't want to get too personal here, but sometimes in the middle of the night, when my wife and children are fast asleep, I make a midnight Oreo run. I'll sneak into the kitchen, slowly and carefully open the food cabinet, and pull out a bag of Oreos that I have previously and surreptitiously planted in the back of the cabinet behind the cans of asparagus. I then get myself a glass of milk, and slowly, carefully, and as quietly as possible (so Claudia doesn't catch me) open the bag of Oreos and eat about a dozen of the black and white treats.

I then sneak back into bed with a smile on my face and sugar in my tummy.

There, I've confessed it. My Oreo sin.

But if a California lawyer has his way, my Oreo-munching days may be over. And all because of one really crummy lawsuit.

San Francisco lawyer Steven Joseph recently filed a lawsuit against Nabisco, the manufacturer of Oreo cookies, seeking a court order that the cookies be banned because they pose a "hidden danger" to the public, particularly to children. Accordingly to the lawsuit, the hidden danger is "trans-fatty acid," a substance that the United States Food and Drug Administration has concluded is hazardous to my health.

The anti-Oreo litigation is the latest in a series of non-fat lawsuits against fast food defendants such as McDonald's, Burger King, Wendy's and Kentucky Fried Chicken.

And the anti-fat lawsuits go nicotine-stained-hand-in-glove with the class action lawsuits against the Marlboro Man and other tobacco manufacturers.

But attorney Steven Joseph claims that his lawsuit to ban Oreo cookies is different from the lawsuits against Ronald McDonald and the Marlboro Man. Joseph claims that while we consumers all know that tobacco and Big Macs are bad for us, we have no idea that Oreos are fattening. Joseph claims that the Nabisco Company has cleverly hidden this fact from you, me and millions of other pudgy consumers that have become addicted to Oreos.

Well, I believe Attorney Joseph has stopped litigatin' and gone to meddlin'. It's one thing to tell Ronald McDonald his coffee is too hot or to tell the Marlboro Man to quit blowing smoke in my face. But when a California lawyer goes after my Oreos … well he's gonna have a fight on his hands!

With all due respect to the cookie-bashing counselor, his lawsuit is based on a faulty premise, specifically that those of us who eat Oreos have no idea the cookies are fattening.

Now I'll admit that I don't know what a trans-fatty acid is. I'm not a nutritional expert, and I don't eat cookies on TV. But while I wouldn't know a trans-fatty acid from a multi-district class action lawsuit, I am well aware of the fact that Oreos are fattening. And how do I know this? Simple. THEY TASTE GOOD! I'm no Nabisco rocket scientist, but even Jethro Bodine knows that if something tastes good, it must be loaded with fat! That's why it tastes good, Bubba!

Moreover, I and every other Oreo-munching American know that if we eat too many Oreos, we're gonna get fat. We don't need the Food and Drug Administration or a California lawyer to explain that to us. I know that Oreos are fattening just like I know that it's not a good idea to drive around town with a cup of steaming hot coffee sitting between my legs. And I didn't learn this from reading a report from the Food and Drug Administration.

We live in a world of warnings. If you buy a pack of cigarettes, you will read on the side of the package that the Surgeon General has determined that smoking can kill you. If you buy a cup of coffee at

McDonald's there are big letters on the side of the cup telling you that the coffee is hot, so don't stick the cup between your legs. And I wouldn't mind at all if the next time I was ripping open a package of Oreos at midnight, I read the following warning on the side of the package: "Warning: Eating Oreos will cause your stomach to become approximately the same size as the State of Texas!"

But warnings apparently aren't good enough for Attorney Joseph. He believes you and I and millions of other fat consumers are so stupid we won't heed warnings. So he wants a court order that simply takes away our cookies.

Well, here's a warning to Attorney Joseph: Counselor, be careful what you pray for. Your lawsuit threatens more than my Oreos. It threatens your cookies as well. In fact, it threatens the legal cookies of you, me and every other lawyer in America. Why? Simple. Advocates of tort reform are going to jump on your lawsuit faster than I can rip through a package of Oreos.

U.S. Supreme Court Justice Potter Stewart once said, "I can't define pornography, but I know it when I see it." Well, similarly, we Oreo-lovers may not know trans-fatty acid when we eat it, but we sure know stupid lawsuits when we see them. If you succeed in taking away our Oreos, we consumers may get thinner, but you're going to get a lot poorer if tort reform is passed by Congress and the state legislatures. And don't think it will never happen. When we voters don't have our cookie-fix, we do crazy things like calling our congressmen and demanding our fair share of trans-fatty acids. You've heard of pork barrel legislation? Well, trust me, counselor. That will pale in comparison to the tort reform rush you will see when every member of Congress tries to bring cookies rather than pork back to his or her constituents.

Besides, counselor, we all know what you're up to. Just because we're fat, doesn't mean we're stupid. You may claim that you're out to promote public health, but we all know you're just in this lawsuit for the dough. You've definitely got your hand caught in the cookie jar this time.

And you will never win, counselor. Even if you succeed in getting a court order against the Nabisco Company, I and millions of my fellow Oreo-munching Americans are willing to be held in cookie-loving contempt of court. We will do whatever we have to do to get our trans-fatty acid fix. If Oreos get banned, we'll simply buy them on the black and white market.

I for one will give up my Oreos to a California lawyer only when they pry my cold dead hands off the package.

• • •

Coming Soon:
Regis Philbin Stars in the Trial of the Century

During the 20th century, there were numerous jury trials that were each dubbed by the national media as "The Trial of the Century." These included the infamous monkey trial (*State of Tennessee v. John Scopes*), the O.J. Trial I (*People of the State of California v. O.J. Simpson*), the O.J. Trial II: The Sequel, (*Estate of Nicole Simpson v. O.J.*), and my personal favorite, the Three Stooges trial (*Heirs of Curly and Larry v. Heirs of Moe*).[1]

The 21st century is just a few years old. Nevertheless, I already have my nomination for the trial of this century: *Hugemongous British Insurance Company v. Who Wants to be a Millionaire.*

Recently, the London-based insurance company that insures the hit TV quiz show "Who Wants to Be a Millionaire" filed a lawsuit in Britain's High Court of Justice. The British insurance company claims that its contract with Buena Vista Entertainment Inc., the quiz show's producers, should be set aside because the questions on the quiz show are too easy, and the contestants are winning way too much money.

Under the insurance contract, the British underwriters are required to pay prize money to the show's contestants who win more than a half million bucks. However, the obligations of the insurance company don't kick in until the quiz show has met its deductible of $1.5 million. I don't know who is paying the deductible. Maybe Regis Philbin. Maybe Kathy Lee. Apparently when they entered into the contract, the brilliant insurance underwriters in London were hoping that the quiz show would feature dumb contestants answering very difficult questions. I guess they hoped Who Wants to be a Millionaire would be like a spelling bee in which Dan Quayle was required to spell "onomatopoeia."

Or maybe they thought "Who Wants to be a Millionaire" would have a grand prize winner about as often as the Publisher's

Clearinghouse Sweepstakes.

But unfortunately for the poor insurance company in London, "Who Wants to be a Millionaire" has featured either really smart contestants or really dumb questions or both. In the first two months that the show was on the air, two contestants won a million bucks apiece by answering such difficult questions as "Who is buried in Grant's Tomb?" and "How long was the tour supposed to be for the ill-fated cruise ship on Gilligan's Island?"

Three other contestants have each won a half million dollars by correctly answering such challenging questions as "Who were the stars of the hit TV series, Rocky and Bullwinkle?" and "What type of animal was prominently featured in the Broadway hit musical Cats?"

British barristers for the plaintiff insurance company claim that one does not have to be a rocket scientist to answer the questions on "Who Wants to be a Millionaire." In fact, they claim that most of the questions could be correctly answered by Jethro Bodine.

Well, in all immodesty, I'm something of an expert on the subject of TV quiz shows. I grew up watching such intellectually stimulating game shows such as "The Price is Right," "Truth or Consequences" and "Let's Make a Deal." And take it from me, my fellow dumb Americans, the questions on TV quiz shows are supposed to be easy. If they weren't, nobody would watch the shows.

Take for example the highly popular TV quiz show, "Hollywood Squares." The contestants on "Hollywood Squares" are so feeble-minded that rather than answering the questions themselves, they defer to such intellectual giants as Charo, Whoopie Goldberg, or Judge Judy.

It is true that back in the 1950s TV quiz shows such as "Twenty-One" and "The $64,000 Question" briefly featured such noted eggheads as Dr. Joyce Brothers and Charles Van Doren. However, after a Congressional investigation established that many of the quiz shows were rigged, TV networks soon developed the modern TV quiz show format featuring really dumb people answering really easy questions.

Take for example the quintessential TV quiz show of the polyester decade of the 1970s, "The Newlywed Game."

"The Newlywed Game" was hosted by Bob Eubanks, a man who would never be mistaken for Albert Einstein. In fact, Bob Eubanks made Jethro Bodine look like Albert Einstein.

But Bob Eubanks was a Rhodes Scholar compared to the contestants on "The Newlywed Game." Fittingly enough, the contestants were all newlyweds who were asked to answer difficult questions regarding the events of their wedding nights. These contestants were so stupid they weren't even required to give correct answers to the questions. To win, all they had to do was to give the same answer as given by their spouse. If the husband and wife were both equally dumb, they would still win the prize money so long as they gave the same stupid answers.

When "The Newlywed Game" faded from our TV sets in the early '90s, it was replaced by the equally cerebral "Wheel of Fortune," starring Pat Sajak and Vanna White, a couple who would never be mistaken for Charles Van Doren and Dr. Joyce Brothers. To be a contestant on this show, the only thing you really have to know is the difference between a vowel and a consonant.

The only quiz show in the history of American television to feature smart contestants and tough questions is "Jeopardy!" For nearly 40 years, "Jeopardy!" has been an oasis in the intellectual wasteland of American television. Unfortunately, the show has caused millions of otherwise sensible Americans to put all of their answers in the form of a question.

For example, recently a client of mine who was visiting me in my office asked, "Where is the men's room?"

Inexplicably I responded, "What is the second door down the hall on the left?" My client must also be a big fan of "Jeopardy!," because he then responded, "That's right! And how much did he wager?"

Well, given the fact that I grew up watching "Perry Mason" and TV quiz shows, I sure hope Court TV televises the upcoming "Who Wants to be a Millionaire" trial. It would be like watching "Perry Mason" make a guest appearance on "Truth or Consequences."

One can just imagine what the trial of *Hugemongous British Insurance Company v. Who Wants to be Millionaire* will be like. Who knows? Maybe Monty Hall will be called as an expert witness. Maybe Kathy Lee will testify as a character witness for Regis.

And maybe, just maybe, Regis himself will take the stand as the star witness for the defense. Wouldn't you love to watch Regis's testimony? Why if some Oxford-educated, powdered wig-wearing, prissy British barrister asks Regis a really tough question on cross-examination, Regis will just calmly say, "I think I want to call my lifeline on this one."

And then Regis will place a long-distance phone to one of his really smart friends like Miss America or even Bob Eubanks, and the correct answer to the question will be forthcoming.

Or perhaps Regis will say to the barrister, "You know, I believe I know the answer to your question. I studied this very subject at Notre Dame. But you know, a half million dollars is a lot of money, so I'm going to stop right here."

No doubt about it, *Hugemongous British Insurance Company v. Who Wants to be a Millionaire* will be the trial of the century. And it will culminate at that dramatic moment when Britain's High Court of Justice announces its verdict. And we all know what will happen then. Regis will calmly look at the Judge and ask, "Is that your final answer?"

• • •

1. For more on this intriguing case, see my scholarly article "Why Didn't They Televise the Three Stooges Trial?" *Tennessee Bar Journal* (January/February 1995).

Caskets 'R' Us v. Tennessee Board of Funeral Directors: An Open and Shut Case

It was an open and shut case all the way. And now that the judge has ruled, I might just go out and buy myself a Big Orange casket.

A federal judge in Chattanooga recently ruled that a Tennessee law allowing only licensed funeral directors to sell caskets is unconstitutional. The judge's decision marked the death knell, so to speak, for a casket monopoly. Moreover, it may signal the birth of a new industry in discount and designer caskets.

The issue arose last year when discount casket stores opened in Chattanooga and Knoxville. The stores offered bargain prices on caskets and urns. And with the price of funerals these days, when it comes to dying, a penny saved can definitely be a penny urned.

The Tennessee Board of Funeral Directors and Embalmers did not take this matter lying down. Faced with the specter of discount casket stores called "Caskets 'R' Us" or "Sam's Wholesale Casket Club," the Board of Funeral Directors and Embalmers ordered the stores closed because the stores' owners didn't have a funeral director's license.

The stores' owners were clearly mortified that their new business might be dead on arrival. So they hired some real live lawyers who proceeded to take dead-aim at the Tennessee law giving funeral directors a casket monopoly.

Well, the lawyers for the discount casket companies definitely urned their fees. They persuaded the good judge that the Tennessee legislature should never have undertaken the enactment of the law in the first place.

Now that the funeral directors' monopoly is dead and buried, we casket consumers have a wide range of options.

For example, a casket company in (where else?) East Tennessee has offered a line of "SEC Football Fan Caskets." These are caskets in the official school colors of the Tennessee Vols, the Arkansas Razorbacks, the Alabama Crimson Tide, and other members of the Southeastern Conference.

The caskets feature the official SEC team logo, tastefully emblazoned on a white velvet panel inside the casket lid.

I've read that the cost for such a skybox is $2,000, which is more than the cost of season tickets, but we're talking eternity here, sports fans.

Now prior to the judge's ruling last week, the only way you could get a tasteful Big Orange or Crimson Tide or Arkansas Razorback casket would be to purchase one from a funeral director. But there were two problems with this approach. First, according to the judge's ruling, funeral homes were marking up the price on caskets as much as 600%, making the cost of a Big Orange casket out of this world.

And second, since the SEC casket had to be purchased from a funeral director, we football fans could not buy our own casket but would have to depend upon our widows to buy them for us after we fly away. Well, I know my wife loves me, but I seriously doubt that after I die she will ever look a funeral director in his solemn eyes and say, "I'd like to buy my husband a Big Orange casket."

But behold, Bubba! Yea though we walk through the valley of the shadow of death, we should fear no expensive caskets. We football fans can now go ahead and buy our own SEC discount caskets so that they will be ready for us when the roll is called up yonder!

Just think, when the final quarter ends in the great game of life and you and I head for that big dressing room in the sky, we can remain true to our school. We'll fly away to the tune of Rocky Top.

Although I hope it is a long way off, I can already imagine my Big Orange funeral. My orange and white casket will be carried to a checkerboard grave site by six pallbearers wearing orange and white bib overalls. This will give a whole new meaning to the bumper sticker that reads, "Vol Fan on Board."

My buddy Mark is a big Alabama fan. And when I say big, I mean big. He's about the same size as Freddy Kitchens. Well, when the fourth quarter finally ends for Mark, I know he will want us to send him to meet the Bear in a black and white checkerboard porkpie casket, the eternal Roll Tide model.

Unfortunately, the ruling in *Caskets 'R' Us v. Tennessee Board of Funeral Directors* comes too late for a lot of my friends and loved ones. My late Uncle Earl loved the Georgia Bulldogs. It's a shame we didn't get the chance to put him away in a red and grey discount casket emblazoned with a sign that read, "How 'Bout Them Dawgs?"

Now you may be one of those fans who believes that heaven can wait. But brothers and sisters, you never know when the game of life is about to end. There are no two-minute warnings. It may be later than you think. The half-time show may long be over, and you and I both may be late in the fourth quarter with no timeouts left.

I'm not taking any chances. I'm going to be ready when my sudden death overtime takes place. I'm going to call today and place my order for my Big Orange coffin.

And while I'm at it, I'm going to see if Big Orange Caskets 'R' Us can also offer me a discount designer tombstone. It will be shaped like a goalpost, and on the cross bar will be my epitaph, "I've Gone to Rocky Top. And if You Don't Like It, You Can Go to Gainesville!"

• • •

PART II:
THIS AIN'T YOUR FATHER'S
BAR ASSOCIATION ANYMORE

The Feminization of the Profession, or How To Handle a Speeding Ticket in Arkansas

A majority of America's first-year law students are now female. You read that right, Bubba. Law school graduation day will soon look like a Junior League convention. (The dean will probably get several nice hand-written thank-you notes.)

The young women who comprise the class of 2006 will enter an increasingly-feminine profession. The most recognized judge in America these days is neither Chief Justice Rehnquist nor Judge Wapner. She's Judge Judy.

Let's face it, Bubba. This ain't exactly our father's Bar Association anymore.

Well, I'm no Alan Alda. I'm not even a sensitive Alpha male (whatever that is) like Al Gore. And if my wife ever tells me she's moving to New York to run for the United States Senate, I may hire a female divorce lawyer.

Nevertheless, my male ego is not in the least bit threatened by the fact that a meeting of the associates in my office looks like rush night at a sorority house. I like female lawyers in general, and I love one in particular.

For the past 24 years, I have slept with a female lawyer. We haven't been living in sin; we've been living in Memphis (although I admit that it's sometimes hard to tell the difference). The female lawyer I have been sleeping with is my wife.

For the past 24 years, I have been the husband of a lawyer. I'm not only a member of the Tennessee Bar Association; I'm a member of the auxiliary.

I'm also the son-in-law of a female lawyer. That's right. My mother-in-law is literally a mother-in-law.

Moreover, my wife is not just a lawyer, she's a judge. Her actual title is Shelby County Juvenile Court Referee, but she doesn't wear a black-and-white striped shirt and blow a whistle. She wears black robes and can throw a guy's fanny in jail faster than you can say "dead-beat dad."

Accordingly, the most important people in my life are women who are lawyers. Therefore, the feminization of the profession doesn't bother me at all. It's absolutely fine with me if the Tennessee Supreme Court someday looks like the starting line-up for the Lady Vols basketball team. I think Chamique Holdsclaw would make a great chief justice, and although Pat Head Summit is not a lawyer, she'd make a wonderful governor.

I have a lot of adventures in my life as the spouse of a female judge. One of the more interesting ones occurred a few months ago when Her Honor and I were driving up Highway 63 in rural Arkansas to our family cabin in Whitewater country.

My wife was driving, and I have to tell you that while my wife has taken an oath to uphold the law, she does not always obey the speed limits of Tennessee or Arkansas or any other state for that matter. In fact, very few people know this, but my wife is a graduate of the John Ford driving school.

Well, my wife was in the driver's seat of the family minivan, and we were cruising up Arkansas Highway 63 sort of like Jeff Gordon heading for the checkered flag or Senator Ford heading to Nashville.

Unfortunately, one of Arkansas's finest, (a state trooper who just a few years ago was probably handling sorority visits for the then-governor), saw us as we whizzed by, and so he turned the blue lights on and pursued us.

My wife pulled over, and being the man of the house, I got out on the passenger's side of the minivan and headed back to talk to the trooper.

Now since my wife is a judge, she has these special judicial license plates that identify the owner of the minivan as a judge. Apparently this Arkansas trooper had noticed this when he pulled us over because the first thing he said to me was, "Well, Judge, how you doing?"

My wife was still sitting in the minivan, and so it was obvious to me that I was the one the trooper was addressing as "Judge."

I paused, thought about this for a second, and then replied, "Well, I'm doing fine."

The trooper then said to me, "Judge, is that the little lady sittin' up there in the driver's seat?"

I was tempted to respond, in the words of the great Justice Henny Youngman, "That's no little lady, that's my wife."

But instead, I said, "Yeah, that's the little lady alright."

The trooper then said, "Judge, do you think you could order her to slow down a little bit?"

At this point, feeling more than a little guilty, I said, "Officer, I've got to be honest with you. That little lady is the judge in our household."

And the trooper said, "Man, ain't that the truth! I've got the same problem in my house!"

• • •

Lawyer Barbie Loses Her Appeal

For over 40 years, Barbie has been one of the most glamorous women in the world, living a life most women can only dream about. For example, Barbie has pursued a number of fascinating careers. If you don't believe me, just stop by Toys 'R' Gonna Cost You a Fortune this weekend and browse through the Barbie department. There you will find Ballerina Barbie, Beauty Queen Barbie, Cheerleader Barbie, TV News Anchor Person Barbie, Large Animal Veterinarian Barbie, Investment Banker Barbie, Gorgeous Lady of Wrestling Barbie, and Proctologist Barbie.

Barbie also owns more glamorous merchandise than you can find in the studio of a TV game show. She lives in Barbie's Dreamhouse, drives Barbie's Sports Convertible, works out at Barbie's Health Spa, relaxes in Barbie's Hot Tub, and has a wardrobe more extensive than that of Nancy Reagan and Imelda Marcos combined.

Barbie also has a loving man in her life, a handsome plastic doll named Ken, whom she has dated since the Eisenhower Administration.

No doubt about it, Barbie has led a charmed life.

But recently, for the first time in her toy-filled life, Barbie had a setback. That was the day that Lawyer Barbie lost her appeal as the United States Supreme Court turned down Barbie's request to review a federal court of appeals decision in the case of *Mattel v. MCA Records*. At issue was a 1997 dance song called "Barbie Girl." The song was recorded by a Danish band called Aqua (which should not be confused with the Swedish band ABBA, or the American cologne Aqua Velva), and included the memorable lyric, "I'm a blonde bimbo in a fantasy world."

When Dancing Queen Barbie first heard the line nearly six years ago, she was highly offended. She reportedly cried on Ken's plastic shoulder for over a week.

You see, Barbie is definitely a blonde, but she's no bimbo. In fact, you can search high and low at Toys 'R' Gonna Force You into Bankruptcy without ever finding "Bimbo Barbie."

While Barbie is blonde and has a bust that prevents her from seeing her tiny little plastic feet, she should never be confused with Anna Nicole Smith. (After all, Ken is not a 90-year-old billionaire who made his fortune in the plastics industry.) In fact, Barbie is a college graduate. If you don't believe me, go to Toys 'R' Impossible to Assemble and buy Cheerleader Barbie. So help me, she comes with her own diploma.

And so, the highly intellectual Barbie was highly offended by the song "Barbie Girl" and its explicit message that Barbie is just a bimbo glitter girl.

Being the determined, perseverant modern woman that she is, Barbie struck back. She went to law school, became Lawyer Barbie, and filed a lawsuit on behalf of her manufacturer, Mattel, against MCA Records, the recording company that produced "Barbie Girl" and sold 1.4 million copies of the offensive song.

Unfortunately, when she went to court, Lawyer Barbie came face-to-face with another tough woman, First Amendment Sally, counsel for MCA Records. First Amendment Sally convinced a lower federal court that the "blonde bimbo" reference in "Barbie Girl" was a parody protected by the constitutional right of free speech.

Undeterred, Lawyer Barbie appealed the adverse decision to the United Supreme Court in the hopes that the same people who put President Dubya in the White House might give her redress for being labeled a blonde bimbo.

But like Al Gore, (who now that I think about it, looks an awful lot like Ken), Lawyer Barbie lost her appeal in the nation's highest court.

Even as you read these words, the Danish band Aqua is busily exercising its First Amendment rights by crooning about Barbie the blonde bimbo.

Well if you know Barbie like I do (and as a father of 9-year-old girl, I definitely know Barbie), you realize that she will overcome this setback. Next Christmas season, when you walk into Toys 'R' Gonna Make Your Credit Card Bill Exceed the National Debt, you'll see the newest version of Barbie. She'll be wearing a beautiful set of black robes and holding a tiny gavel. Move over, Sandra Day O'Connor! It's time for United States Supreme Court Justice Barbie!

• • •

Miss America Needs a Lawyer

Here's some advice for Miss America: Honey, you better hire a lawyer. It looks like you're headed right down the runway to a New Jersey courtroom. Before you know it, you'll be named Miss Defendant.

Over the last few weeks, the Miss America Pageant has been spinning out of control much like one of those fiery batons contestants often twirl during the talent competition.

It all started when the Board of Directors of the Pageant announced that, on the advice of its lawyer, pageant rules were being changed so that in the future the competition would be open to women who have been divorced or who have had abortions.

For the past 49 years, the Miss America Pageant has required that all contestants swear that they have never been married nor pregnant. That's right, folks. Miss Mississippi has always had to swear to the judges at the Miss America Pageant that she has never been Mrs. Mississippi or, for that matter, the proud momma of a future Miss Mississippi.

But in an effort to comply with anti-discrimination laws in New Jersey, the home state of the Miss America Pageant, the pageant Board of Directors announced it would rescind this requirement and open up the competition to divorced women and women who have exercised their constitutional rights pursuant to *Roe v. Wade*.

Pageant directors announced that the competition would still ban married women or women who have had children. In other words, Hillary Clinton couldn't compete in the pageant as Miss Illinois or Miss New York or Miss Arkansas even if she divorced Bill. It's just too late for Mrs. Clinton. She eliminated herself from the competition over 20 years ago when she had Chelsea.

Well, faster than you could say "Miss Congeniality," the Miss

America Pageant found itself in court. The director of the Miss Kentucky Pageant filed a lawsuit to stop the Miss America Pageant from changing the rules.

This lawsuit was quickly settled as the Miss America Pageant Board of Directors agreed to rescind the rules changes and continue to ban mommies and divorcees from the competition.

While this ended any hopes some of us had of someday seeing Elizabeth Taylor in the swimsuit competition, it was also hoped that this would be the end of Miss America's legal problems. Well, not so fast, accordion-breath!

Given the fact that the whole purpose of the rules changes was to comply with the New Jersey anti-discrimination laws, it's just a matter of time before some divorced momma in New Jersey takes Miss America to court.

Now I'm not a constitutional lawyer, and I don't play one on TV. Furthermore, I have no expertise whatsoever regarding either beauty pageant law or New Jersey anti-discrimination law. However, it seems to me that millions of American mommas and divorced women clearly have a cause of action against the Miss America Pageant for discrimination.

Just because some poor gal discovers shortly after her honeymoon that her husband is not exactly Mr. Congeniality does not mean that she should be banned for life from the Miss America Pageant. Hey, who's to say that a divorced woman can't look just as great as a single woman in a bathing suit and high-heeled shoes?

And where is it written that a divorced woman can't play Lady of Spain on the accordion with one hand and twirl a baton with her other hand just like the other single gals do in the talent competition in the Miss America Pageant?

No doubt about it, a divorced woman is just as capable as a single woman to put a crown on her precious head and walk down a long runway while simultaneously smiling like Nancy Reagan and crying like Tammy Faye Baker.

And what is the legal basis for excluding mommas from the competition? Now I can understand why a pregnant woman might be banned from the pageant. After all, a pregnant Miss Alabama wouldn't have a chance in the swimsuit competition. Besides, it wouldn't be safe to have pregnant woman walking down the runway in high-heels.

But for the life of me, I can't understand why a woman who's had a baby should not be allowed to compete for the position of America's "ideal woman." You can never convince me that had June Cleaver divorced Ward, she would not be fit to be Miss America.

And while I pray that my wife will never divorce me, if she does, I do not think she should be banned from competing for the title of Miss America just because she and I have had three kids.

The truth of the matter is my wife looks great in a swimsuit and high-heeled shoes. However, in nineteen years of marriage, I've never seen her wear both items at the same time.

Besides, my wife doesn't play the accordion.

Don't get me wrong. I have no intention of suing Miss America either on behalf of my wife or any other similarly situated mommy in America.

But there is no doubt in my mind that a lawsuit is coming, and Miss America needs a lawyer and she needs one now. Why before you know it, the entire Miss America Pageant will be converted from a beauty pageant to a class action lawsuit on behalf of divorced women and mommies across America.

Next year's competition won't be hosted by Regis or Kathy Lee or Donny or Marie. It will probably be hosted by Court TV's Marsha Clark.

The judges for the event will be the New Jersey Supreme Court.

And don't be surprised if pursuant to a court order, the five final-ists in next year's competition will be Mrs. New Jersey, Miss

Mississippi Momma, Miss Divorced Montana, Ms. Pro-Choice Pennsylvania and Mr. Hawaii.

It's enough to make you long for the good old days when the Miss America Pageant was all about swimsuits, not lawsuits.

• • •

A Princess Dreams of Becoming a Lawyer

Nearly fifty years ago, a young woman from Greeneville, Tenn., was admitted to the University of Tennessee College of Law. As a first-year law student, she was not exactly greeted with open arms. During her very first week of law school, she was confronted by the law school dean who told her in no uncertain terms, "You're not welcome here, ma'am. We all know you are only here to find a husband."

Despite this inauspicious beginning, the young woman stayed. And to borrow a line from William Faulkner, she not only endured; she prevailed. Three years later, she was one of two women in the University of Tennessee College of Law of 1948.

She married one of her classmates. Years later she would graciously joke, "The dean thought he had been right about me all along since I did find a husband at the law school."

She and her husband moved to a little town in the mountains of southeast Tennessee. There she continued to face adversity. Like Justice Sandra Day O'Connor, her first job was as a legal secretary because the gentlemen's club that was the Bar at that time would not hire her as a lawyer.

She eventually hung out her shingle in a storefront office in the small town and practiced law there for over 40 years.

Along the way, she and her husband had a little girl. They named her Claudia.

In 1977, following in her mother's footsteps, Claudia entered the University of Tennessee College of Law. But unlike her mom, Claudia had many female classmates. In fact, over a third of her class was female.

I was present for Claudia's graduation from law school on a warm spring day in 1980. And a year later, on May 23, 1981, I played a very small role in Claudia's wedding. I was the groom, which meant in order of importance, I ranked at best, fourth behind Claudia's mother, Claudia, and the caterer. On cue, I said those two magic words ("I do!"), and a few seconds later, I was pronounced to be the husband of a lawyer and the son-in-law of two lawyers, including that woman from Greeneville, Tenn., who had courageously entered law school shortly after the end of the Second World War.

Claudia and I now have three children. The youngest is a little girl named Margaret Grace. I call her "The Princess."

I recently asked The Princess what she wanted to be when she grows up. Without hesitation she said, "I'm going to be a mommy lawyer."

Well, I know I'm a proud daddy and therefore I'm not impartial. But I predict that in about 20 years, The Princess' dream will come true. After all, The Princess has quite a legacy.

• • •

PART III:
ANDY, ATTICUS AND ME

Andy of Mayberry, Esquire

My dad is a big fan of Matlock, the fictional TV lawyer who bears a striking resemblance to a former law enforcement official from North Carolina. Although Matlock, the TV series, was canceled years ago, Dad still watches Matlock every night unless the Braves are playing. Dad can thank Jane Fonda's ex-husband for that.

The former Mr. Jane Fonda, a/k/a Ted Turner, is the owner of WTBS, the cable "Superstation" in Atlanta.

My dad gets 348 cable channels, including ESPN, ESPN-2, CNN, C-SPAN, the Golf Channel, Court TV, the Home Shopping Network, and the Jerry Falwell Network. But Dad doesn't watch any of these channels. The only channel he watches is the Former Mr. Jane Fonda Superstation channel. Why? Simple. The Former Mr. Jane Fonda Superstation channel only broadcasts two shows, specifically Atlanta Braves baseball or reruns of "Matlock."

Dad doesn't mind at all that these are the only shows broadcast by the Former Mr. Jane Fonda Superstation channel. They are the only shows Dad wants to watch. In fact, it would be a dream come true for Dad if one summer night he tunes into the Former Mr. Jane Fonda Superstation channel and sees Matlock hit a home run in the bottom of the 9th to win the game for the Braves against the evil Barry Bonds and the San Francisco Giants.

Dad and I talk most every day, and when we do, he always asks me one of the following two questions:

1. Did you see the Braves last night?
2. Did you see Matlock last night?

Sometimes rather than asking me one of these two questions, he asks the rhetorical question, "How 'bout them Braves?" or "How 'bout that Matlock?"

Matlock is Dad's all-time favorite lawyer. He likes Matlock more than Perry Mason, Johnnie Cochran, Judge Wapner and Greta van Weiss all put together.

My dad has never seen me try a case either live or on TV. He's not going to see me on the Former Mr. Jane Fonda Superstation channel either, because I never made a guest appearance on "Matlock." But my dad is absolutely convinced that it would help me as a lawyer if I would watch re-runs of "Matlock." Dad's always saying things to me like, "Son, you should have seen the closing argument Matlock made last night!"

Or he'll say, "Boy, that was really something the way Matlock solved that crime last night."

My dad is a retired Baptist preacher, not a lawyer. Therefore, he has no appreciation of the "reasonable doubt" defense. He likes Matlock because every night (except when the Braves are playing) Matlock proves the innocence of his client by doing what O.J. Simpson is now trying to do. Specifically, Matlock always finds the real killer and brings him to justice.

Moreover, Matlock, like Perry Mason before him, generally exposes the real killer right in the courtroom during the trial. That's because for reasons I can't figure out, whenever Matlock is defending a case, the real killer attends the trial and is sitting in the audience in the courtroom. I guess he just wants to make sure he got a way with the crime.

For many years, Dad has encouraged me to watch Matlock. I'm sure he thinks that watching the show would make me a better lawyer.

Dad may be right, but I just can't bring myself to watch "Matlock." Why? Well don't tell this to my dad, but I refuse to watch "Matlock" for the simple reason that if I watched it, it would spoil my all-time favorite TV show, "Andy of Mayberry."

When it comes to television, my dad and I do have something in common. We're both fans of Andy Griffith. But while Dad is a fan of Andy Griffith Matlock, the lawyer, I'm a fan of Andy of Mayberry, the sheriff.

Just as Dad enjoys watching re-runs of "Matlock," I love to watch re-runs of "Andy of Mayberry."

"Andy of Mayberry" was set, fittingly enough, in the fictional town of Mayberry, North Carolina. The great American philosopher Lyndon Baines Johnson once said that there are several towns in America too small to support one lawyer, but there is not one town in America too small to support two lawyers.

Well apparently the great LBJ never visited Mayberry. To my knowledge there was no Mayberry Bar Association because Mayberry did not have a single lawyer.

The fictional town of Mayberry had representatives from virtually all other occupations other than the legal profession. There was Sheriff Andy, Deputy Barney, Floyd the barber, Emmet the small appliance repairman, Goober the mechanic, and Gomer the Marine.

There was also Otis the town drunk, Aunt Bea the domestic engineer, Helen Crump the educator, Juanita the diner waitress, and Opie the student.

But there was not one lawyer in the whole town. No one ever defended Otis on charges of public drunkenness. No one represented Barney in litigation against Gomer for a false citizen's arrest.

"Andy of Mayberry," like "Matlock," was canceled years ago. But it lives forever in syndication. Just as my dad happily spends his evenings watching either Andy Taylor Matlock or the Atlanta Braves, on most evenings I can spend a carefree half-hour with my old friends, Andy, Barney, and even Ernest T. Bass. And knowing Ernest T. as I do, I can tell you that he sure could have used a good lawyer.

I've always refused to watch "Matlock" because I'm afraid it would just confuse me. Andy Griffith will always be Sheriff Andy Taylor to me, and I just could not sit through an episode of "Andy of Mayberry, Esquire" without grabbing the remote control. If I watched Andy Taylor try a jury case, I would just get hopelessly confused. I would ask myself, how did this happen? Did Andy marry the ambitious Helen Crump who then insisted that he head to Chapel Hill for law school?

Maybe Howard Sprague became a lawyer, and he and Andy learned the wisdom of LBJ that while Mayberry was too small to support one lawyer, there was a whole lotta money to be made by two lawyers!

Well, listen, I'm sorry but I've got to go. Dad just called. The Braves have the bases loaded in the bottom of the ninth and Bobby Cox has just decided to pinch-hit Matlock for Chipper Jones.

● ● ●

Atticus Finch Loses in Muskogee, But Wins in Chicago

A sk a lawyer to name his or her favorite book and the odds are the response will be *To Kill a Mockingbird*. It is the inspirational story of Atticus Finch, a country lawyer who lost his biggest case.

Well, unfortunately poor Atticus has lost again, only this time he lost in Muskogee, not Maycomb.

The great American philosopher Merle Haggard once proudly crooned that Okies from Muskogee "don't smoke marijuana down on Main Street." Well, apparently those Okies from Muskogee also don't let their kids read great books.

The school board in Muskogee, Okla. voted to ban *To Kill a Mockingbird* from the public school's reading list. The school board's verdict: *To Kill a Mockingbird* is guilty of the charge of being politically incorrect.

The evidence? The school board found that the "N" word appears frequently throughout the book. Therefore, *To Kill a Mockingbird*, like Mark Twain's famous racist work, *Huckleberry Finn*, was deemed "offensive" to African-American students.

Never mind that the "offensive" language of the novel was not the language of Atticus Finch or Harper Lee, but rather the language of the racists who denied Tom Robinson justice.

Never mind that the inspirational message of *To Kill a Mockingbird* is that heroes like Atticus Finch battle racism, ignorance, and injustice.

All that went for naught in Muskogee, just as it did in Maycomb.

Once again, Atticus lost.

Once again, justice did not prevail.

But don't despair, Atticus! You may have lost in Maycomb and

Muskogee, but it looks like you're going to be a winner in Chicago!

That's right, Atticus, Chicago! The City of Big Shoulders! The Windy City! The town that Billy Sunday couldn't shut down!

Chicago is a city that has always recognized and celebrated heroes. Michael Jordan. Ernie Banks. And more recently, Sammy Sosa.

And this month, the City of Chicago will celebrate the greatest lawyer hero of all time, Atticus Finch.

Chicago Mayor Richard Daley has asked all Chicagoans to read *To Kill a Mockingbird* as part of the city's annual library week celebration. There will be group discussions of the book in libraries, coffee houses, book stores and private homes throughout the city.

The Chicago Bar Association is going to join in the celebration by re-enacting Tom Robinson's trial. I for one hope they bring Gregory Peck back for closing argument.

When the good people of Chicago read the book and when the Chicago Bar Association re-enacts the trial of the *State of Alabama v. Tom Robinson*, the book's final chapter and the jury's verdict will not change.

But that doesn't mean Atticus will be a loser.

He wasn't really a loser in Maycomb.

He wasn't really the loser in Muskogee. (The children in the Muskogee public schools were the losers.)

And he wasn't a loser when he first walked into my life at the "picture show" 37 years ago.

And so here's to Boo Radley and Reverend Sykes and Scout and Jim. Here's to Gregory Peck. Here's to Mayor Daley and Oprah and Sammy Sosa and all the good people of Chicago.

And most of all, here's to a remarkable woman named Harper Lee who over 40 years ago gave America a hero named Atticus Finch.

• • •

A Vote for Bill is a Vote for Pork!

I have never run for or held public office. I've never served as sheriff or court clerk or dog catcher, and I have not spent one day of my life on the public payroll.

Actually, I did hold statewide office for a few days back in 1969 when I was in the 11th grade and was selected as Frayser High School's representative to Boys State. This meant that I got an all-expense paid trip to Cookeville, Tenn. where I spent a week living in one of the palatial dorms at Tennessee Tech University.

Every delegate to Boys State is "elected" to some statewide position. There's a Boys State Governor, a Boys State Lt. Governor, a Boys State Treasurer, etc.

I was named Boys State Commissioner of Insurance and Banking. I was sort of a 16-year-old Jake Butcher.

I served for four days as Boys State Commissioner of Insurance and Banking until I was indicted by the Boys State Attorney General for bank fraud.

Fortunately for me, I got a pardon from Boys State Governor Lamar Alexander, and I caught the first bus back to Memphis.

But with the exception of that week in Cookeville some 30 years ago, I have never been in public life.

I have never served a term in either the legislature or the state penitentiary.

Frankly, I've never felt qualified to hold public office. I am not a wrestler nor a movie star nor a preacher, and I don't even own a plaid shirt.

I'm neither a Lincoln nor a Ford.

I am a life-long member of the male gender, and proud of it. But I am not now, nor have I ever been, an alpha-male.

But despite my total lack of qualifications for public office, I have decided that the time has come for me to throw my hat (actually my Vols cap) in the ring.

My fellow Tennesseans, I am announcing today my candidacy for the position of … Tennessee Secretary of Barbeque!

Now before I start getting phone calls from any pointy-headed state bureaucrats, let me acknowledge that I realize that the State of Tennessee currently does not have a Secretary of Barbeque. But that's the very reason I am launching this important statewide campaign. You see, my fellow pig-loving Tennesseans, I sincerely believe that we Tennesseans need to move quickly to create the position of Secretary of Barbeque before Tennessee is once again beaten by Florida.

Believe it or not, the Florida legislature is now considering a bill to create the position of Secretary of Barbeque in the Sunshine State. According to the bill, the Secretary of Barbeque would be responsible for promoting "the uniqueness and diversity of barbeque in Florida."

It is a classic example of pork barrel legislation.

As a life-long, pig-eating Tennessean, I can't stomach the idea of Florida beating us out in the creation of this important public office. Florida can have Steve Spurrier and Mickey Mouse, but those Gators have no bidness whatsoever holding themselves out as ambassadors of barbeque.

Whoever heard of Florida barbeque? Heck, it's an oxymoron.

Have you ever eaten a barbequed orange? And let's face it, absolutely no one takes a vacation in Florida's Redneck Riviera in order to eat barbeque.

But we Tennesseans know barbeque. Barbeque is the most important natural resource of the Volunteer State, and folks in Florida or any other state for that matter can't hold a rib to Tennessee's barbeque.

Accordingly, we Tennesseans need to move quickly to create the position of Secretary of Barbeque before Jeb Bush appoints America's first Ambassador of Pork.

And here is where, in all immodesty, I come into the picture. My fellow Tennesseans, read my sauce-covered lips: Tennessee needs a Secretary of Barbeque, and I AM THAT MAN!

I was born and raised in Memphis, the barbeque capital of the world. I have spent over 50 years in River City eating the world's greatest barbeque, and I have the cholesterol count to prove it.

I've also dined at every great barbeque joint in the State of Tennessee. I've eaten pork shoulder at Bozo's in Mason, the pig salad at Lewis' in Moscow (Tennessee, not Russia), and ribs at the Rendezvous in General Washburn Alley in downtown Memphis.

But not only have I spent nearly a half century eating Tennessee barbeque; I am a world-class barbeque cooker as well.

For many years, I served as captain of the Legal Loins, one of the premier teams competing in the Super Bowl of barbeque cooking, the Memphis in May Barbeque Cooking World Championship. The Legal Loins was a team of lawyers who excel not only in the courtroom but at the barbeque pit as well.

While I and the other members of the team have now retired and hung up our aprons, I still proudly wear my official Legal Loins tee-shirt emblazed with our official team logo (a gavel-wielding pig) and the official team motto ("The hog, the whole hog, and nothing but the hog!").

And so I am ready, my fellow pig-chomping Tennesseans, to serve as the Volunteer State's first Secretary of Barbeque. I am willing to shoulder, so to speak, the awesome responsibilities of this new public office.

I am willing at great personal sacrifice to tirelessly travel across the great State of Tennessee from Memphis to Mountain City and stop at every rib shack and barbeque pit I can find. I will pay any price, bear any burden, and eat any pig for the cause of Tennessee barbeque.

To borrow a line from Franklin Delano Roosevelt, I believe I have a rendezvous with destiny. And a Corky's, too.

And so my fellow swine-lovers, I ask for your prayers, your votes, and more importantly, your ribs and shoulders and wings.

Ask not what your country can do for you, ask what you can do to help me become Tennessee's first Secretary of Barbeque.

And remember my campaign slogan: A vote for Bill is a vote for pork!

•   •   •

Flying the No-Longer-Friendly Skies

'm so old I actually remember when flying on a commercial airliner was a very enjoyable experience. I took my first flight in 1956, when I was only four years old. My mother and I flew a Southern Airways DC-3 from Memphis to Atlanta. Nearly a half century later, I still vividly recall every moment of the flight.

Mom and I boarded the DC-3 by climbing up a small step ladder through a door at the end of the plane, right by the tail section. Once inside the plane, we were greeted by a very happy, smiling stewardess (they weren't called flight attendants in those days) who treated us as if we were royalty. She escorted us uphill to our seats, given the fact that even when a DC-3 is on the ground, it juts up at 45° angle. (Think of the plane Humphrey Bogart put Ingrid Bergman on at the end of Casablanca. That was a DC-3. Fly it again, Sam!) Our seats were first class, but that's not because we were rich. (Remember, folks, my daddy was a Baptist preacher.) All seats on a DC-3 — all 20 of them — were first class.

Before we took off, the stewardess handed me a package of Chiclets. She told me to chew them during the flight so that my ears wouldn't pop. Also, before the flight, Mom and I were personally greeted by both the captain and the co-pilot, who told us that the weather was nice and they were certainly happy that we were flying with them to Atlanta, thank you. The captain even presented me with my very own set of pilot's wings that he pinned to the lapel of my suit jacket. (Mom had dressed me up in my Sunday School clothes for the flight.) After pinning the wings on me, the captain pronounced that I was "an official Southern Airways junior pilot!" Mom took a picture of me shaking hands with the captain. (Just a couple of us flyboys ready to take off!)

After we were airborne and reached cruising altitude, the stewardess hooked trays to our seats. In those days, the trays did not flip out of the seat in front of you. The stewardess then brought us a wonderful hot lunch served on real china on real linen with real silverware. Mom and I dined as if we were Queen Elizabeth and Prince Charles.

After lunch, the stewardess escorted me to the cockpit so that I could enjoy a brief visit with the captain and co-pilot. Even though I was an official Southern Airways junior pilot (Captain Billy!), I was not allowed to fly the plane.

When we landed in Atlanta, the captain, the co-pilot, and the stewardess walked Mom and me downhill to the back of the plane and helped us out the door and down the step ladder. The entire crew then reiterated how much they appreciated that we had flown with them. Mom and I thanked them profusely for getting us safely to Atlanta so that I could visit with my grandmother. Then, Grandmother herself made a dramatic appearance, racing from the Atlanta airport gate to the side of the plane where she hugged Mom and me, and then took a picture of Mom, the stewardess, the captain, the co-pilot and her grandson, Captain Billy.

Fifty years later, I am now a frequent flyer. Several times a month, I fasten my seatbelt, make sure my seatback and tray table are in their full, locked and upright position, and soar off into the once-friendly skies. More often than not, I am still flying from Memphis to Atlanta since there are a lot of mean doctors in Atlanta who like to testify against the nice innocent doctors I represent in Tennessee. Besides, as the old joke goes, whether you're going to Heaven or Hell, you're probably going to have to change planes in Atlanta. But take it from me, flying from Memphis to Atlanta is not what it used to be. These days commercial air travel is about as exciting and romantic as a cattle call.

First, when you get on airliner these days, you are not greeted by a happy, smiling stewardess. Instead, you encounter a grumpy flight attendant who has all the charm of a Marine drill instructor. If you ask her any questions, she's most likely going to tell you to sit down and shut up.

Second, unless you are prepared to take out a second mortgage on your home, you will not be flying first class. You will be flying "coach," which should not be mistaken for second class or even third class. In coach you will be surrounded by people who are approximately the same size as Japanese Sumo wrestlers. And once you reach cruising altitude and the "fasten seatbelt" sign goes off, these wrestlers will spend the rest of the flight climbing over you during their repeated trips to the bathroom.

Third, you will no longer be served a hot meal on real china with real linen and real silverware. If you're lucky, you will receive a package of peanuts and a bottle of warm tap water.

And believe it or not, it's getting worse. Recently, the annual Airline Quality Rating Study was released, containing the shocking finding that the "overall quality of air travel is deteriorating" these days. Fewer flights are on time, complaints about air service are up 27%, and airlines are laying off employees and cutting back on services. The good news is that there's not much more cutting back that the airlines can do. There are no more hot meals or junior pilot wings. American Airlines recently got rid of blankets and pillows on flights. The airline claimed that it was a cost-reducing measure to save $300,000 a year. I think American Airlines was just trying to avoid an inevitable pillow fight between disgruntled customers and grumpy flight attendants.

I sure wish Southern Airways was still around and offering DC-3 service from Memphis to Atlanta. I've been told that a modern jetliner flies at twice the speed of a DC-3, but I don't believe it. When Mom and I flew from Memphis to Atlanta 50 years ago, the wonderful flight took off on schedule, arrived on time, and seemed to last just a few joyous minutes. But these days when I am crammed between two Japanese Sumo wrestlers inside a modern Delta jetliner at the Memphis airport, the plane proceeds to taxi halfway to Atlanta where it sits on the tarmac for an hour before finally taking off on a bumpy, miserable flight that seems to last forever.

Maybe rather than just complaining, I ought to do something about this. After all, I am still an official Southern Airways junior pilot.

• • •

Runaway Humor Columnist Has Time to Kill

J ohn Grisham and I have so much in common. We're both lawyers. We both have written and published books. And we've both had book-signings at the coolest book store in the world, Burke's Book Store in Memphis. But I'm afraid the similarities end there.

John Grisham has sold over 60 million books. I've sold about 12, and that's counting the nine I bought for myself. Grisham's books appear on the *New York Times* Best-Seller lists. My books have been sold in stores that sell the New York Times. Well, that's not exactly right. My books have been offered for sale at stores that sell the New York Times, but I can't say for sure that anyone ever actually bought a copy. However, I'm hoping that one of these days a book of mine will appear on the Best-Seller List under the category, "Non-Fiction Authored by a 52-Year-Old Lawyer from Memphis Named Bill."

Over the past 16 years, John Grisham has come to Memphis every February and had a book-signing at Burke's. Literally thousands of people have stood in line for hours to get a signed copy of one of Grisham's best-selling legal thrillers such as *The Firm*, *The Client*, *The Pelican Brief*, *The Pelican Boxer Shorts*, *A Time to Sue*, and my personal favorite, *The Honest Young Lawyer Who Beats the Huge Dishonest Memphis Law Firm that is Controlled by the Mafia*.

I had a book-signing at Burke's a few years ago and, like Grisham, I had a long line of customers in front of me. Unfortunately, that was because I had stationed myself in front of the store exit in a desperate attempt to get people to buy a copy of my book. It got kind of ugly, especially when I told an old lady that she couldn't leave until she bought a copy of my book and asked me to sign it. ("Just buy a copy, lady, and nobody gets hurt!") Corey and Cheryl Mesler, the store's owners, had to quickly intervene and politely insist that I leave. I agreed to do so, but only after I bought five copies of my book and signed them for myself. ("To my good friend and number one fan, Bill, from your idol, Bill.")

For the past 16 years, John Grisham's annual appearances at Burke's have been the hit of the Memphis literary season. Each year on February 1, Grisham has appeared at Burke's like a literary groundhog. Literate Memphians see Grisham's shadow and realize we have six more weeks of winter reading ahead of us. But I recently read in the Burke's Book Store Newsletter that this February, Grisham will not be making an appearance at Burke's. Instead, he's sending 2,000 signed copies of his newest book, *The Broker*, which will no doubt soon appear on the *New York Times* Best-Seller List after everybody in America buys a copy to take to the beach this summer. I know when I make my annual non-book-signing appearance at the Redneck Riviera this summer, I'll be clutching my copy of *The Broker* in one hand and a tube of sun block in the other as I take my kids to the beach.

The Burke's Newsletter did not state why Grisham will be a no-show this February. Maybe he's too busy working on his next best-seller, *The Runaway Jury that gets Chased by Mobsters and Runs Off to a Tropical Island with Tom Cruise and Julia Roberts*. But whatever the reason, I feel bad for Corey and Cheryl and all Memphis readers who look forward to Grisham's annual River City homecoming. I feel so bad that I'm going to publicly make a very generous offer to Corey and Cheryl Mesler. I'm willing to come to Burke's and serve as John Grisham's stand-in for a book-signing. I'm even willing to counter-sign the 2,000 copies of *The Broker* that John has already signed. Under John's signature, I will simply add, "and Bill Haltom!"

There is only one thing I request in consideration of my generous offer. I want every customer who buys a signed copy of *The Broker* to also buy a signed copy of one of my books. And to sweeten the deal, I'm even willing to forge John Grisham's signature on each and every purchased copy of my own book.

This could be the beginning of a great new February tradition at Burke's Book Store: The Grisham-Haltom Signing!

And Corey and Cheryl, I make you this promise. No matter how successful I become, I will come back every February. I will never miss a Grisham-Haltom book-signing. And also, I promise I'll stop that business of blocking the exit door.

• • •

PART IV:
DRESS FOR LEGAL SUCCESS

A Classic Summer Law Suit

'm an old-fashioned, traditional Southern lawyer. I talk like a
Southern lawyer, walk like a Southern lawyer, and dress like a
Southern lawyer. And so on Tuesday morning, June 1 (the day after
Memorial Day), I put on my summer law suit.

When I say "summer law suit," I'm not referring to hot litigation.
I'm making a fashion statement. Literally.

A summer law suit is your classic cotton seersucker suit. Blue and
white striped. And don't forget the shoes. White bucks, like Pat Boone
wore in the '50s. And if you really want to look the part, you can top it
off with a straw boater hat, although you really need to be a cool
country lawyer to pull this off.

My wife calls my seersucker suit and white bucks my "Matlock
outfit" because it is the same wardrobe that Sheriff Andy Taylor wore
to court every day after he left Mayberry, went to law school, moved to
Atlanta, changed his name to Matlock, passed the Georgia bar, and
became a lawyer.

It's getting harder and harder to find a good classic seersucker suit
these days. Most men's clothing stores don't carry them anymore.
Instead of seersucker and summer poplin, men's stores now sell "year-
round, medium-weight suits."

I hate year-round medium-weight suits. They are a fashion abomina-
tion. If a southern man wears medium-weight suits 365 days a year, he is
going to sweat to death in the summer and freeze to death in the winter.

But for we lawyers who live below the Mason-Dixon Line, the
summer seersucker suit is not a luxury. From Memorial Day to Labor
Day, it's a necessity.

I order my "Matlock" suits from either Joseph Bank or Brooks
Brothers, and I wear them throughout the summer for four reasons.

First, I wear them because when I was a little boy, my dad wore them. Dad has always been my role model, and even though I'm now 52 years old, I still try to dress like my father.

Second, I wear them because they weigh about an ounce and are the only comfortable suit a southern lawyer can wear when the temperature is 95 degrees, the humidity is 97%, and the heat index is roughly the same as Ted Williams' lifetime batting average.

Third, I wear a summer seersucker suit because you really don't have to worry about keeping it pressed. A seersucker suit always looks wrinkled. It's supposed to look wrinkled. When I show up at my office or the courthouse on summer mornings dressed like Matlock, it makes no difference whatsoever that I look like I slept in my suit. A seersucker suit is wrinkle chic.

And finally, I wear seersucker suits because I am a trial lawyer, darn it. Litigators may sit in their air-conditioned offices wearing medium-weight Eye-talian suits while they take depositions or bate-stamp documents. But we trial lawyers go to court and try cases. And when we present ourselves to a jury in the summertime, folks expect us to look like Matlock. I don't care if the courthouse is air-conditioned. I want to stand in front of the jury in cotton seersucker, gloriously wrinkled, and fanning myself with one of them funeral home fans, just like Clarence Darrow did at the Scopes trial in Dayton.

So from now until Labor Day, when the southern fashion police dictate my seersucker goes back in the cedar closet, I'll be wearing my featherweight, eternally wrinkled, always-in-summer-style law suit and my "April Love" white bucks.

Go ahead. Call me Matlock, and snicker if you will while you perspire in your medium-weight Armani suit. You may think my summer outfit is hopelessly out of date, but that's no sweat off my back. I'm telling you, when I wear my seersucker suit, I am one cool lawyer. Literally.

• • •

Where Will Clark Kent Change His Clothes?

ere is some bad news for mild-mannered reporter Clark Kent and his alter ego, Superman. Clark, the next time you are ready to become the man of steel, you might have trouble finding a place to change your clothes. And it's all because every lawyer in Metropolis now has a cell phone.

The Bellsouth Corporation, better known as "the phone company," recently announced that it is going to shut down all 143,000 of its pay phones by the end of next year.

Over the past several years, pay phones in general and phone booths in particular have increasingly become an endangered species, sort of like bald eagles, moderate Baptists, and liberal Democrats. In fact, since 1996, the phone company has shut down over a half million pay phones and phone booths across the United States. And now, with Bell South's decision to close its entire fleet of pay phones, the ancient phone booth is about to go the way of the dinosaur. By the end of next year, the only place you will be able to find a phone booth in America will be the Smithsonian Institution.

The death of phone booths is a direct result of what I believe was truly the worst invention of the 20th century — the cellular telephone.

An estimated 90 million Americans (including 900,000 lawyers) are now spending virtually every waking hour of the day talking non-stop into little black mobile telephones pressed against the sides of our collective national faces. Thanks to cell phones, we Americans are now constantly yakking like a bunch of magpies. We yak into our cell phones as we walk down city sidewalks. We yak into our cell phones while we drive down country roads. We yak into our cell phones as we wait in line for our fast food lunches. We yak into our cell phones while sitting in theaters waiting for the movies to start. And some rude folks yak into their cell phones even after the movie begins.

Worse yet, some people are actually talking into their cell phones during church services. I was recently sitting in church during, of all things, a funeral service, when suddenly a cell phone rang a few pews behind me. I half expected the church organist to start playing, "Operator, Information, Get Me Jesus on the Line!" But now that I think about it, I seriously doubt that my cell phone-toting brother a few pews behind me was talking to the Lord. To my knowledge, the Lord doesn't even have a cell phone. He doesn't need one, and besides, the roaming charges would be out of this world.

Above all, we yak into our cell phones while we are driving our cars in rush hour traffic, posing a clear and present danger to the other cell phone-yakking drivers who share the road with us.

Thanks to cell phones, you and I do not have one moment of peace and quiet. We are now accessible not only when we are in the office, but when we are in our cars, on airplanes, in bass fishing boats, at church, or at football games. We've all become like the late President Lyndon Baines Johnson, who used to conduct important matters of presidential business by phone while sitting in the presidential john.

Actually, we're not even conducting any serious business by cell phone. The only thing people do on cell phones is announce where they are at any given moment. "Hi, honey! It's me! The kids and I are watching the movie! Julia Roberts is terrific!"

"Hi, honey! It's me again! I'm here at Earl's funeral! They did a good job on old Earl. He really looks like himself!"

"Hi honey! I'm on my way home! I'm gonna be a little late. Just rear-ended the guy in front of me."

Well, as if all this cell phone yakking isn't bad enough, the decision by the phone company to shut down all pay phones and demolish the few remaining phone booths could set off the biggest crime wave in the history of Metropolis.

At this very moment, mild-mannered reporter Clark Kent is sitting next to Don Paine and me in the newsroom of the TBA *Daily Planet* helping me crank out this column. What if Clark gets a call on his cell phone alerting him that Lex Luther has kidnapped Lois Lane?

Now that the phone company is demolishing all the phone booths, where in the world will Clark Kent put on his blue Superman jersey, red cape and matching red leotards?

• • •

Some Mighty Big Pumps to Fill

There are many reasons that I am thankful to be a man. At the top of the list is the fact that I don't have to wear women's shoes.

For the past 24 years I have lived with a woman, specifically, my wife. For the first few years of our marriage, we shared a closet. Sharing a bed is nice. Sharing a closet is not. Closet cohabitation is probably the number one cause for divorce in America. And so finally, to save our marriage, my wife and I agreed to a legal separation … of our clothes.

But despite the fact that my wife and I got separate closets years ago, I still make visits to her closet from time to time in search of a runaway sock or a pair of boxer shorts. Men's underwear just can't stay away from women's underwear.

Based on my occasional visits to my wife's closet and my constant observation of her feet, I've become something of an expert on women's shoes. My wife is no Imelda Marcos, but like most women, she does have several pairs of shoes. For nearly a quarter century, I have observed my wife's shoes on a daily basis, either in the closet or on her feet. And based on my non-scientific study, I have reached the following conclusions about women's footwear:

1. Women's shoes have to be the most uncomfortable item of clothing designed in human history since Eve first started wearing a fig leaf. Please don't get me wrong. I've never worn a pair of pumps in my life, and I don't intend to. As far as I am concerned, women's shoes are mighty big pumps to fill. I can tell by looking at these contraptions that they have to be about as comfortable as a rectal exam.

2. Women's shoes cannot be good for the feet. I'm not a podiatrist, and I don't play one on TV. But you don't have to be Dr. Footmeister to recognize the toll women's shoes take on feminine feet. If you don't believe me, just take a look for yourself. Go ahead. Just sneak into your

wife's closet and examine any shoe from the 700 pairs she owns. Just notice the structure of this podiatric torture chamber. All five toes must be jammed together into a pointy tip about the size of your pinky. The rest of the foot must then jet upward at a near 90 degree angle, culminating in a tourniquet-type strap that chokes the ankle. The whole effect is to make your wife approximately the same height as Shaquille O'Neill, which supposedly makes her more beautiful. And then the poor gal has to walk around all day in these cosmetic stilts that cut off all blood circulation above the knee.

3. Women's shoes are coyote-ugly. I have never seen an attractive pair of women's shoes. The current fashion is the Wicked Witch of the West shoes. Women all over America (including, unfortunately, my wife) are walking around these days wearing pointy-tipped shoes that could kill a cockroach in the narrowest of corners. When I first saw my wife wearing this latest heeled fashion statement, I immediately asked, "So where is you black hat and your broom?" She did not think this was funny.

We menfolk wear ugly shoes, too. Each day when I go to the office, I wear my Air Nixons, ugly black wingtips. And when I come home at night, I slip on a pair of sneakers I have owned since the first Reagan administration. My old Air Nixons and Air Reagans are about as attractive as my wife's Air Wicked Witches. But when a guy is wearing a pair of Air Nixons, he doesn't have to walk around all day looking like a cross between a ballerina and the Leaning Tower of Pisa.

All this reminds me of the wisdom of the former Governor of Texas, Ann Richards, who once said, "Fred Astaire wasn't the greatest dancer in history. Ginger Rogers was. She did every dance move Fred did, except she did it backwards wearing high heels."

• • •

Will Living in Sin Mean Death to Lawyers?

Ever since we lost the Civil War, we Southerners have been behind the times. We were the last folks in America to get such modern amenities as indoor plumbing, electricity, air conditioning, karaoke and sushi bars.

But in recent years, Jed and Granny and Jethro and Elly May and the rest of us folks down here in Dixie have been playing catch-up with Yankees and other sophisticated folks from around the country. Why if you don't believe me, go visit Atlanta. The place has become so sophisticated that when you are there, you don't even realize you're in the South. In fact, Atlanta is so modern it now looks just like Cleveland.

Not so long ago, the Southern landscape was filled with cotton fields and magnolia trees. On hot summer nights, the Southern sky was illuminated by the flashing tails of lightning bugs.

But there are now casinos in the cotton fields of northern Mississippi. There are gleaming office towers soaring across newly-urbanized landscapes from New Orleans to Charleston. And on hot summer nights, you can no longer see lightning bugs in the Southern sky. They've been obscured by the bright lights of big Southern cities. Besides, there are no lightning bugs inside domed stadiums or suburban shopping malls.

When I was a little Southern boy growing up in Memphis in the 1950s, my granddaddy used to tell me, "Son, some day the South is gonna rise again!"

Well, it did, but not in the way Granddaddy envisioned.

And now, thanks to the 2000 U.S. census, we have the most compelling evidence to date that the South really has caught up with modern America. Are you ready for this, Bubba? We Southerners are now catching up with rest of America when it comes to living in sin!

You read that right, Wanda June! According to the most recent U.S. census, the number of unmarried couples co-habitating grew faster in the South over the past decade than in any other part of the country.

And while Southern cohabitation is on the uprise, Southern marriages may soon be gone with the wind. Tennessee and Arkansas — the home states of Bill Clinton and Al Gore — now rank second and third nationally in divorce rates.

Guess which state has the highest overall proportion of unmarried couples? Florida. This should come as no surprise. After all, Mickey Mouse and Minnie have been living in sin in Orlando for decades.

But this proliferation of Dixie cohabitation may be bad news for us Southern lawyers. In the short term, it may mean more divorce cases. But in the long term, the wages of all this living in sin could be death. The death of the legal profession, that is.

Why? Simple. We lawyers make a living off sin, but only surreptitious sin.

The bread and butter of the legal profession is people who get caught with their pants down, both literally and figuratively. But when the day comes that folks sin openly and notoriously with no shame, there will be absolutely no need whatsoever for lawyers.

You see, when Adam and Eve were naked in the Garden of Eden, they had no need for a lawyer. But once they ate from the Tree of Knowledge, they suddenly went from being "naked" to being "nekkid." It was the late, great theologian Lewis Grizzard who explained the difference between "naked" and "nekkid." "You are naked," explained Brother Lewis, "when you don't have any clothes on. But you're 'nekkid,' when you don't have any clothes on, and you're doing something you're not supposed to be doing." Well once Adam and Eve went from "naked" to "nekkid," shame came into play. And once people started being ashamed, they needed lawyers.

And that's why this recent trend of living in sin, Southern-style, is a threat to Southern lawyers.

Sin is nothing new in the South. We Southerners were major-league sinners long before major league baseball came to Atlanta. It's just that we used to sin on the sly and with style. That was the really cool thing about Southern sin. We were sinners, but we pretended to be honorable ladies and gentlemen.

Take, for example, drinking. Long after Prohibition ended across America, most Southern counties remained "dry." That is to say, liquor was illegal. But do you think this meant that good old boys and Southern belles sipped only iced tea? Absolutely not. Liquor flowed across the dry counties of the South like the Mississippi flows towards New Orleans. As the late, great Will Rogers once wrote, "Every election day, the voters of Oklahoma stagger to the polls and vote dry!"

And who were the beneficiaries of all this drinking in Southern dry counties? The bootleggers and us lawyers, that's who.

And how about carousing? Hey, a whole lot of that went on too, but we Southerners never did it out in the open. We Southerners fooled around with a lot more class than did Prince Charles or President Clinton.

All this carousing down in Dixie was great for Southern lawyers. What was important to us lawyers was that all those folks who were secretly getting nekkid wanted to be viewed in public as honorable.

We all knew it wasn't the case. For example, in our Southern hearts, we knew that Scarlett was appropriately named and that Rhett was a scoundrel. But they didn't shack up at Tara. They actually got married and pretended to be honorable, even though the wedding ceremony didn't convert Scarlett into Melanie or Rhett into Ashley.

But if openly living in sin now starts spreading across the South like sexual kudzu, Atticus and the rest of us Southern lawyers might as well close up shop.

It is one thing for us Southerners to enjoy such Yankee amenities as air conditioning, hockey games and designer coffee houses. But if we now start jettisoning such great Southern institutions as marriage, honor and a good old fashioned sense of shame, we lawyers are in real trouble.

You see, these days old Bubba and Wanda June aren't only living in the new South. They're living in sin! And when they're living in sin, they're not co-habitating with lawyers!

• • •

Brother, Can You Spare Ten Bucks for a Cup of Coffee?

Not so long ago in America, panhandlers would stop folks on the street and ask, "Brother, can you spare a dime for a cup of coffee?" But don't be at all surprised if in the near future you are approached by an economically distressed homeless person who asks, "Sister, can you spare ten bucks for a cup of Starbean's tall café latte cappuccino espresso mocha java supremo? And while you're at it, could you spare another five bucks for a bottle of Norwegian designer spring water?"

I'm a coffee addict. Each morning when I arrive at my office, I am immediately greeted by my litigation team — Della, Paul, and Gertie. The four of us sit down in my conference room and each enjoy a cup leaded, high-octane caffeine coffee before we begin another day of zealously representing my innocent clients.

Throughout the workday, I enjoy several more cups of coffee. In fact, I've seriously considered putting a coffee I.V. line beside my desk so that I can have caffeine continuously pumped into my system while taking phone calls.

I've always admired coffee for its simplicity. It's just a basic black drink that I make every morning in the same Joe DiMaggio Mr. Coffeemaker that I bought when I was in law school 25 years ago.

But while I still drink coffee every day, I'm not sure I understand it. You see, coffee, like so many other things in American life these days, has suddenly become incredibly complicated.

First, coffee has become incredibly complicated to buy. In the old days, I would just go to the grocery store and buy the brand of coffee that I had seen Danny Thomas advertise on TV. For many years, Danny

Thomas was America's foremost expert on coffee. He was always appearing on my TV screen doing commercials for a brand of coffee that he told me was "good to the last drop." And on his TV show, "Make Room for Daddy," Danny was always doing coffee "spit-takes," as he would actually spray coffee on his wife and children and co-stars whenever he would receive some startling news.

Well, Danny's gone to heaven now. At this moment, he's probably doing a spit-take with St. Peter and Joe DiMaggio.

But without Danny's guidance, I don't know what coffee to buy.

Second, coffee has become incredibly complicated to make. I still have my Joe DiMaggio Mr. Coffee coffeemaker, and it works fine. But all my upscale friends now have more coffee gadgets than Juan Valdez. They grind environmentally friendly Guatemalan recycled virgin coffee beans in fancy machines they buy at fancy stores such as the Sharper Upscale Image. When it comes to coffee, if my wife and I are going to keep up with the Rodham-Jones's next door, we're are going to have to buy our own designer industrial strength coffee grinders and home espresso makers. Where have you gone, Joe DiMaggio? You and Mr. Coffee have left and gone away and have been replaced in American kitchens by Ms. Café Latte.

But worst of all, it has become incredibly complicated these days simply to order a cup of coffee. Faster than you can say "Seattle's Best cinnamon grande cappuccino," designer coffee houses are sprouting like mushrooms across the American landscape.

When I was a boy, coffee houses were found only in exotic, sophisticated places like Greenwich Village, San Francisco or Brentwood, and they would be frequented only by beatniks like Maynard G. Krebs from the old "Dobie Gillis Show." Maynard and his buddies would sip coffee while reciting poetry and playing bongos.

But these days you can find designer coffee houses in such

beatnik-free places as Memphis, Tupelo, Ootewah and Etowah.

And when you walk into your neighborhood designer coffee house, don't expect to find a cup of coffee. Instead, be prepared to shell out several bucks for something called a tall grande supermissimo café cappuccino. And when you get your grande mochamaxima latte, don't dare dunk a donut in it, or you're likely to be tossed out of the coffee house on your designer fanny.

Also, when you are in a coffee house, be very careful about ordering a glass of water. It may cost you another five bucks. Believe it or not, designer coffee houses not only sell designer coffee. They also sell designer bottled water with fancy names such as "L'Aqua du Norway" or "Le Water de Pepe Le Pew." They claim such water comes from underground French springs or Norwegian fjords. I'm actually thinking about starting my own line of West Tennessee bottled water. I'm going to call it "L'Aqua du Wolf River."

Well, here's hoping my Joe DiMaggio Mr. Coffee maker lasts another 25 years. When it breaks down, I'll have no alternative but to switch to hot tea.

• • •

PART V:
GEEKS, GADGETS AND GIZMOS
(NOT TO BE CONFUSED WITH THE LAW FIRM BY THE SAME NAME)

The Geeking of the Profession: Slowly But Surely, We're All Becoming Techno-Nerds

've always enjoyed the company of lawyers. You show me a really good lawyer, and I'll show you a fascinating person who enjoys life and is fun to be around.

One of the reasons I am a Bar junkie is that I just like to hang out with lawyers. I like to drink with lawyers, break bread with lawyers, and share war stories with lawyers.

I like to vacation with lawyers, play golf with lawyers, and go to Vol football games with lawyers.

My dearest friends are lawyers, and for the past 24 years, I've slept with a lawyer. (IMPORTANT NOTE TO MY WIFE: I'm talking about you, dear.)

Heck, I even like to be around tax lawyers, although I did hear someone once say that you'll never know the meaning of the word "boring" until you meet a tax lawyer who is training for his first marathon.

Don't get me wrong. I'm no Will Rogers. I can't say that I've never met a lawyer I didn't like. But my favorite people are lawyers, and what I enjoy most about being a lawyer is the camaraderie of other lawyers.

But brothers-in-law and sisters-in-law, I am concerned about the future of our profession. I'm afraid that many of us, myself included, aren't nearly as interesting or fun as we used to be.

Recently I've noticed an alarming trend, specifically, the geeking of the profession. I blame this trend on modern communications technology.

Based on my extensive research conducted in courthouses and conference rooms across the Volunteer State, I've developed what I call Haltom's Law of Techno-Geek Advancement: There is inverse relationship between the sophistication of a lawyer's gadgets and the quality of that lawyer's personality.

To put it more bluntly, the more sophisticated technological toys we lawyers obtain, the nerdier we become.

If you don't believe me, conduct your own research as follows: Strike up a conversation with a trial lawyer over the age of 50. You'll find it to be a delightful experience. You'll hear colorful war stories about trials or maybe you'll find yourself in an engaging discussion about good books or theatre or the finer points of hunting and fishing. Your conversation will be uninterrupted, unless the trial lawyer offers to buy you a drink.

Now try to strike up a conversation with a litigator who is a carrying a hand-held combination remote internet access PDA pager mobile cell phone. First, you probably won't be able to have a conversation with this lawyer because he or she will be too busy talking into their remote internet access whachimacallit to some other techno-lawyer who, at that very moment, will be about to cause a lawsuit because he is driving 80 miles per hour on Interstate 40 while trying to access the internet on his Blackberry Palm Nimbus 2000.

In the unlikely event that Mr. or Ms. Robo-Lawyer quits talking like Captain Kirk into his Handspring Doohickie VII and finally talks to you, guess what he or she will talk to you about. War stories? No way. Good books or fishing and hunting? Forgetaboutit!

So help me, the only thing Techno-lawyer will discuss with you is his or her new hand-held remote internet access PDA Visor and how it works.

Talk about a fascinating conversation! It will be enough to make you desperately search for a tax lawyer who is training for her first marathon.

This whole trend of the techno-geek lawyer started, innocently enough, with pagers. I still remember the first time I ever saw a lawyer wearing a pager. I was sitting in a deposition back during the Reagan years when suddenly my adversary across the table started chirping like a cricket on speed. I had no idea why he was going off like a smoke alarm.

My chirping adversary then grabbed his crotch and pushed some button to turn off the alarm.

"What in tarnation was that?" I asked.

"My pager," he responded. "I've got to make a phone call."

"Got some client in the emergency room needing a legal bypass?" I asked.

Of course, the days of chirping lawyers are long over. Now modern techno-lawyers wear something called "vibrating pagers." These days I'll be sitting in a deposition asking questions, when suddenly my adversary sitting across from me will smile, sigh softly, and then announce that his vibrating pager is telling him it's time to make a phone call on his remote internet access Raspberry XII.

Again, don't get me wrong. I'm not saying we lawyers shouldn't have cell phones or internet accessors or even vibrating pagers. Frankly, I wouldn't mind having one of those vibrating pagers myself, only I'm afraid I wouldn't know how to strap it on. I sure wouldn't want to shock myself.

But what I am saying is that if we lawyers spend every working hour talking about our gadgets, we'll become about as interesting as your typical CPA, or worse yet, your typical actuary.

Think for a moment about the heroes of our profession. Did they sit around talking about their gadgets? Can you imagine Clarence Darrow saying to William Jennings Bryan, "Hey, Bill, look at my new pen! It's called a 'ballpoint'!"

And how about the great Atticus Finch? Can you envision him interrupting a conference with Tom Robinson so he could use his Palm Pilot to send an e-mail to radleyboo@mockingbird.com?

So I implore you, my fellow lawyers! Let's quit talking about our gadgets! When we get together, let's turn off our cell phones and

Blackberries and Strawberries, and for God's sake, please don't show me your vibrating pager!

Tell me a war story about a colorful lawyer or a judge from days gone by! Talk with me about the Vols or hunting or fishing or that new book about Teddy Roosevelt.

And if you promise me you'll never say a word about your new vibrating Handspring Visor VII, I'll even buy you a drink!

• • •

The Naked Truth About Cell Phones

I hate cell phones. I hate them in the morning when I'm stopped at a traffic light and the guy in the car in front of me is chirping like a magpie into his cell phone, totally oblivious to the fact that the light is green.

I hate cell phones during my lunch hour when they chirp like crickets throughout the restaurant as the folks at other tables take their "urgent" calls ("I'm having lunch at Chez Heartburn. What are you doing?")

I hate cell phones when I'm in a deposition and everybody in the conference room looks like cowboys with their little cell phone holsters strapped to their waists. It's a litigation cell-phone shoot-out as old Wyatt Earp the lawyer and Marshall Dillon the expert witness whip out their cell phones and fire off words to their offices.

I hate cell phones when I'm sitting in a plane on a runway and the guy sitting just inches next to me is chattering away on his cell phone like a chipmunk on speed.

I hate cell phones on weekends when I take my wife to a movie, and invariably, somebody's cell phone starts ringing right during the climax of the film when Governor Schwarzenegger is about to save the planet. (Hasta la vista, cell phone baby!)

I hate cell phones on Sunday mornings when I am sitting in church and one of the brothers or sisters' cell phones goes off during the sermon.

I particularly hate cell phones that play annoying tunes. It's bad enough when they ring, but I'm ready to strangle somebody when I hear cell phones that play the first few bars of a stupid song such as "The Mexican Hat Dance" or "Inna Gadda Da Vida."

Recently I was in a hearing in a Memphis courtroom when a cell phone started ringing. I was confident the judge would hold some lawyer in contempt until, so help me, it turned out the cell that was ringing belonged to the judge! (By the way, he did not hold himself in contempt.)

But if all this isn't bad enough, I've recently discovered one more reason to hate cell phones. Are you ready for this? I hate cell phones because believe it or not, they can now show the world what I look like when I'm buck nekkid. And I admit, it's not a pretty sight. Don't laugh. Your fanny may be exposed as well.

The naked truth about cell phones has recently been revealed, so to speak, in health clubs across America. Increasingly, cell phones now come equipped with cameras that enable users to take pictures and then transmit them to folks who have small screens on their cell phones for their viewing pleasure. So help me, all across the nation, cell phone camera owners have been sneaking their phones into health club locker rooms and showers, surreptitiously taking pictures of naked people, and sending them to cellular voyeurs throughout the world.

Hold on to your towels, folks. The next time you step out of the shower at the Y, well, smile, you may be on candid cellular camera!

To paraphrase a line from the classic film, *Cool Hand Luke*, what we have here is something much worse than a failure to communicate. This is an issue that should not be covered up. If we allow this to continue, we will all be the butt of a serious invasion of privacy. We have to get to the bottom of this issue now. Believe me, this is not something that will simply peter out.

Lawmakers in several states have already banned cell phones from moving vehicles. And now the time has come to get these privacy assault weapons out of locker rooms and showers.

And so I urge you, my fellow lawyers: Go to your cell phones right now, call your Congressman and tell him to do something about the national cell phone-cameras-in-the-showers crisis. But before you do, make sure you are dressed.

• • •

Green Eggs and Spam

Like most 21st century lawyers, I start off each day with a breakfast of spam. It is served to me in heaping e-portions on the screen of my personal computer.

Each morning when I arrive in my office, I log into my personal computer and then spend at least one billable hour reading and deleting spam e-mail that has been electronically delivered to me overnight.

It is absolutely amazing the number of people throughout the world who thoughtfully send me e-mails in the middle of the night. My e-mail buddies fall into three broad categories. First, there are those people around the cyber world who are deeply concerned about my anatomy and my love life to the point where they constantly send me e-mails offering to sell me "natural male enhancement" products. To my knowledge, absolutely none of these people have ever seen me naked. Therefore, I don't know why they have singled me out for a such targeted e-marketing campaign. Nevertheless, I have to admit that the sheer volume of the e-correspondence concerning my need for "natural male enhancement" has absolutely wrecked my confidence. Let's face it, folks. It's a terrible way for a middle-aged lawyer to start his day, reading 47 spam e-mails about his need for enhancing his anatomy, albeit naturally.

My second group of e-buddies consist of deposed royalty in far away countries. Several times each week I get an e-mail from the Crown Prince of Swaziland, advising me that his royal government was recently overthrown in a civil war and that he needs to transfer vast sums of money to my bank account. He indicates he would be ever so grateful if I would simply provide him with my bank account number and the name and location of my bank so that the transfer can take place right away. He also promises that at a later date, he will appear in my office to reclaim his royal booty minus my handsome attorney's fee. Why this e-artist formerly known as Prince has selected me and my bank account out of all the lawyers and financial institutions in America is beyond my e-comprehension. Every morning I keep hitting the delete key, but Prince Valiant keeps sending his "urgent and confidential" e-messages, begging me for my bank account numbers. Only Ed McMahon has sent me more letters promising to make me instant an millionaire.

And finally, there is my third group of e-buddies who serve me spam for breakfast each morning. Believe it or not, these are the anti-spam spammers. These are folks who are so concerned about my e-mail box being overloaded with spam that they send me more spam telling me that they can stop all the spam! These spammers are offering to sell me super-duper spam blockers that will once and for all end my long cyber-nightmare of spam. If I will just buy the super deluxe anti-spammer, I will never again hear from any of my aforementioned e-buddies who are worried about my anatomy or want to transfer their riches to my bank account.

Well pardon my cynicism, but if these guys are losing sleep at night worrying about my spam, why are they sending me anti-spam spam in the middle of the night? And besides, if I sign up for anti-spam super-duper spam blocker, how will my buddy Prince Valiant ever get the royal treasure out of Swaziland?

And once the spam is gone, will I start off each day by deleting all the anti-spam that I'll be getting from my e-buddies proudly announcing that they are successfully blocking the spam?

Well, enough of this spam about spam. I've got to go take my natural male enhancement vitamin pill and then check the balance in my bank account. Quick! Hit the delete button!

• • •

Will a Palm Pilot Ever Beam Me to the Redneck Riviera?

When I was a little boy, one of my favorite TV shows was "The Jetsons." It was the compelling story of a 21st century family consisting of George Jetson, Jane his wife, daughter Judy, his boy Elroy, and his dog, Astro ("Reah-row-Rorge!").

The Jetsons were a futuristic family that enjoyed all the amenities of 21st century life. They had a flying car, television phones, a robot housekeeper (Rosie), and a treadmill for walking Astro. At the end of each episode, poor George would get stuck on the treadmill and would scream out for Jane, his wife.

When I was a little boy, I was confident that someday I would live like the Jetsons. I was convinced that by the early 21st century, I would be flying my space car each morning to my job as general counsel for Spacely Sprockets.

Well, it is now 2005, four years after we were all supposed to have a space odyssey. Frankly, after growing up watching the Jetsons, the 21st century is turning out to be a major disappointment.

Instead of a flying car, Claudia my wife and I have a minivan that looks more like Fred and Wilma Flintstone's car.

Instead of a television phone, Claudia my wife and I have voice-mail. ("This is George Jetson of Spacely Sprockets! I can't come to the phone now, but your call is very important to me ...")

Unlike the Jetsons, we do not have a robot housekeeper. Instead of Rosie the Robot, Claudia my wife has me to take out the trash.

Like the Jetsons, Claudia my wife and I do have a dog and a tread-mill. However, our dog is named Cuddles and unlike either Astro or Scooby-Doo, he cannot talk. ("Reah-row, Rill!") And since I still have vivid memories of what happened to poor George at the end of each of episode of "The Jetsons," I never, absolutely never, walk Cuddles on my treadmill.

No doubt about it, so far the 21st century has been the biggest letdown since, well since Y2K.

But a couple of weeks ago, I thought my space odyssey was finally about to arrive. Claudia my wife asked me if I would like to have as a Christmas gift something called a "Palm Pilot." I had absolutely no idea what a Palm Pilot was. I assumed he was somebody I would hire to fly me to the Redneck Riviera for a fishing trip.

But my 21st century wife and my futuristic son, Elroy, patiently explained to me that a Palm Pilot is an indispensable device for today's modern e-lawyer.

At my wife's urging, I test-drove a "Palm Pilot" that was loaned to me by one of the futuristic young associates at my office. Specifically, I test drove something called a "Palm Pilot III."

From the test-drive, I learned to my disappointment that a Palm Pilot won't enable you to fly to work. In fact, it won't fly you anywhere. It's just a small hand-held contraption similar to what Captain James T. Kirk carried around during episodes of "Star Trek." As you no doubt recall, Captain Kirk would be sitting at the command post of the Starship Enterprise and would flip open his Palm Pilot and use it to dictate his "captain's log."

On other occasions, Captain Kirk would be on some dangerous planet in a galaxy far away and about to be attacked by Klingons. He would whip out his Palm Pilot, press it against his lips and calmly say, "Beam me up, Scotty!"

Well, unfortunately, the Palm Pilot III is not quite that good. I haven't tried out a Palm Pilot V or a Palm Pilot VII, but I can assure you that the Palm Pilot III does not enable one to be beamed up out of trouble. Instead of beaming folks up, the Palm Pilot III serves as an electronic calendar, address book, notepad, and e-mail receiver. Perhaps its most important feature is that it enables a bidness person to play Solitaire during a boring meeting.

Well, having grown up watching "The Jetsons," I have to tell you that I was extremely disappointed with the Palm Pilot III. As far as I am concerned, for the time being, I'm just going to make do with a legal pad, a number two pencil, and deck of cards.

But I still dream that before my life is over, I will live the life of George Jetson, 21st century bidnessman! I hope I will zoom to work each morning in my flying car, or better yet, just stay at home and have a teleconference with my boss, Mr. Spacely. I also hope I live to see the day that my trash will be taken out by Rosie the robotic housekeeper.

And above all, I hope that someday I will hold in my hand a Palm Pilot XXXIII. And when things start to go bad for me during a hostile court appearance, I will just calmly pull out my Palm Pilot XXXIII, press it against my lips, and say, "Beam me up, Scotty!"

•••

The Blog That Ate Dan Rather

University of Tennessee Law professor Glenn Reynolds is a very powerful man. Over the last couple of years he has brought down a Senate majority leader, an executive editor of *The New York Times*, and more recently, Dan Rather. And he did it all while sitting in his pajamas. (His, not Dan Rather's.)

Professor Reynolds is the "King of the Blogs." Now for those of you who, unlike me, are not on the cutting edge of e-journalism these days, let me explain what a "blog" is. A "blog" is a sort of personal website in which the "blogger" writes his or her own little commentaries about the news of the day and refers readers to other news stories and blogs that can be found on the worldwide web. It's a sort of rest stop on the information superhighway where readers can pull over, get gas, and buy the informational equivalent of an RC Cola and a Moon Pie.

Professor Reynolds' blog is called "Instapundit.com," and can be found, surprisingly enough, at www.instapundit.com.

I'm a regular reader of Instapundit.com, and I have to tell you I am absolutely amazed at Professor Reynolds' blogging ability. I understand he has a wife and kids and a full-time job at UT Law School. But despite these challenges, he finds time to post up to 20 to 30 brief commentaries a day on Instapundit.com. starting at about 6 a.m. and ending around midnight. If you don't believe me, just check it out for yourself. The guy really must be working in his pajamas, or at least his boxers.

And never underestimate the power of Professor Reynolds and his worldwide network of fellow bloggers and blog readers, like myself.

A couple of years ago, a fellow named Trent Lott was serving as majority leader of the United States Senate. He was wielding power like Lyndon Baines Johnson and was generally thought to be the second most powerful man in America, right behind Dick Cheney. But then Senator Lott made a terrible mistake. He went to Strom Thurmond's birthday party. It was a grand occasion since Senator Strom was about 150 years old and had served in the Senate since Millard Fillmore was in the White House and God was a little boy. At the birthday party, Senator Lott got carried away, remembering the good old days when Senator Thurmond was just 70 and ran for president on a segregationist platform. Senator Lott proudly proclaimed that he and his fellow citizens of Mississippi had supported Senator Thurmond in his campaign, and golly gee, he sure wished President Thurmond had been able to lead our great country.

Incredibly, the national media did not initially cover the story about Senator Lott's birthday party tribute. Apparently, Tom Brokaw, Dan Rather and Peter Jennings weren't listening. But the Instapundit was. Professor Reynolds went on his blog and said, in so many e-words, *did you hear what this idiot said*?! Suddenly the blogging world was abuzz with the news about Trent Lott, and before you knew it, Dr. Bill Frist was the new Senate Majority Leader.

New York Times Editor Howell Raines was the next big shot to be tried and convicted and sentenced to journalism death in the world blog court after the Jason Blair scandal. (New *New York Times* motto: All the news that's fit to make up.) And then came Dan Rather, anchor person for the "CBS Evening News" with Dan Rather. Last September, Dan aired documents regarding President Bush's service in the National Guard. And mighty powerful documents they were, containing reports that the president was so pitiful in his National Guard Service that he didn't even bother showing up for a physical.

But there was a problem with the documents. They were about as reliable as a Bill Clinton promise of fidelity. Worse yet, they were more than unreliable. They were outright forgeries.

How do we know this? Professor Reynolds and his fellow bloggers told us so. The bloggers, who after all, know something about computers, proved that the CBS documents were the result of computer word processing, not the work of a typewriter. This was a remarkable achievement since the documents were supposedly prepared in 1971, long before Bill Gates invented the personal computer and Al Gore invented the Internet.

After spending several days trying to defend himself, Dan Rather finally appeared on his news program, admitted the documents were a forgery, and, believe it or not, apologized. That's right. Dan Rather apologized. It was the biggest mea culpa since Jimmy Swaggert was caught with his pants down.

Well, I promise you this. I will never get in a fight with Professor Reynolds or any of his fellow bloggers. In fact, I've just been told that Professor Reynolds has just posted a note on Instapundit.com proving that this entire column is a forgery.

As the late, great Jim Croce sang in the '70s in a song he composed on his personal computer, you don't tug on Superman's cape, you don't spit in the wind, you don't pull on the mask of that old Lone Ranger, and you don't mess around with Instapundit!

• • •

Grandmother Never Caught a Snail-Mail Lovebug Virus

Recently, I arrived at my office bright and early to begin another exciting day in my glamorous career as a trial lawyer. After saying good morning to my secretary, Gertie, my paralegal, Della, and my private investigator, Paul, I proceeded to do what I do at the beginning of each day of my glamorous career. I poured myself a cup of leaded, high-octane, non-Starbucks' coffee, turned on my personal computer, and proceeded to check my e-mail.

I hate e-mails. Like the fax machines of the late 20th century, e-mails have created a false sense of urgency for every lawyer, bidnessman and bidnesswoman in America.

Nevertheless, I check my e-mails every morning because my income and my glamorous career as a trial lawyer depend more and more these days on techno-skilled clients who send me several e-messages each day. When the e-mail says jump, I immediately ask (or rather, type), "How high?"

And so, I'm sitting at my personal computer, fat, dumb and happy, when I notice that I have an e-mail with the following intriguing subject line: "LOVE-LETTER-FOR YOU.TXT-VBS."

Well, that was a first. A love-letter e-mail. But what made this more intriguing was that the "from" line of the e-mail indicated that the love letter was from a buddy of my named Tom. Now I don't know whether Tom is an alpha male. However, I do know that he is married to a gorgeous woman named Gwen, he has a daughter named Elizabeth, and like me, he always looks forward to the swimsuit edition of *Sports Illustrated*.

Accordingly, using my brilliant legal mind, I quickly discerned that one of two things was true. Either my buddy Tom had decided to come out of the closet and express his cyberlove for me (unlikely, given Tom's love for Gwen and *Sports Illustrated*), or this love e-mail was some kind of mistake.

The answer came within a few cyberseconds. Suddenly I got a whole series of e-mails warning me not to open any love letters from Tom or even from Tom's wife, Gwen. I was told that if I opened such an e-mail love letter, my computer would catch some sort of Internet lovebug virus. As it had turned out, some guy in the Philippines (not my buddy Tom, by the way) had sent out the e-mail love letters to millions of people around the world, spreading the love bug virus and causing billions of dollars worth of damage.

Well, all this e-mail lovebug commotion has got me to thinking, and I have reached a bold conclusion. It's time to bring back the fountain pen.

During my lifetime I have seen the evolution of communications from snail mail to e-mail. When I was a little boy, there were three basic ways one could send an important message to someone in another part of the world. The first was to write them a letter.

Letter-writing took a lot of time back in the dark ages when I was a boy. You see, we didn't have "word processors" back in those days, so the only way I could "generate" a letter would be to use a fountain pen and a piece of paper.

I wrote an awful lot of letters when I was a boy. I would take my fountain pen in hand and write my grandmother in Georgia and my uncle in Texas. I would also write a number of my "pen-pals" around the country. My "pen-pals" were childhood buddies of mine who had either moved away from my neighborhood or whom I had met at camp or on scout trips.

Letter-writing was a very slow process. It took time to compose my thoughts and put them down on paper. And then it took even more time to put the letter in an envelope, address it, put a stamp on it, put the letter in the family mailbox, and raise the red flag on the mailbox to signal the mailman to pick up the letter.

Not only did letter-writing take a long time. It would take even longer for my letter to make its way to Grandmother in Georgia, or to Uncle Billy in Texas.

The second way one could send a message when I was a boy was by telegram. However, I never met anyone in my life who either sent or received a telegram. I only knew about telegrams because actors and actresses were always getting them in the movies. When I was a boy, the most dramatic moment of any "picture show" would occur when the film's star would receive a telegram announcing the happy ending. With trembling hands, young Andy Hardy would breathlessly share the telegram with his co-star, Judy Garland: "Have read the script for your play, STOP! It is wonderful, STOP! Please catch next plane to New York to begin work on Broadway show, STOP! Or we can just convert the Hardy family barn into a theater, STOP!" (Cast and audience cheer!)

And the final way one could send a message when I was a boy was via carrier pigeon. Again, however, this was only done in the movies. My family didn't even own a carrier pigeon, and not one carrier pigeon ever arrived at our house with a message.

It's been over 25 years since I wrote my last letter to my grandmother in Georgia and my uncle in Texas. They are both in heaven now, and therefore any letter I would send would come back marked (as Elvis used to sing) "return to sender."

I don't write many letters anymore. Instead of writing letters, I dictate them to Gertie who then churns them out on a word processor.

I don't even own a fountain pen anymore. Instead of a fountain pen, I have a dictaphone, voice mail, a cell phone, a fax machine, a

"PC" and e-mail.

I refuse to wear a beeper. I don't want to walk around chirping as if I were a cricket who is rubbing his hindlegs together.

But maybe it's time to turn off the e-mail, shut off the dictaphone, pull the plug on the fax machine, and buy me a brand new fountain pen.

True, when I was a little boy, it took an awfully long time to write my grandmother and tell her I loved her. And it took an awfully long time for an agent of the United States government to transport that letter all the way from Tennessee to Georgia. But one thing's for sure. When Grandmother opened that letter, neither she nor my fountain pen ever caught a virus.

• • •

PART VI:
LITIGATION MEANS NEVER HAVING TO SAY YOU'RE SORRY

The Only Acceptable Apology is a Rectangular One

In 1971, I was a freshman majoring in football appreciation at the University of Tennessee. Through blind, dumb freshman luck, I managed to get a date with a very nice coed, the lovely Wanda June Whipple from Wartburg. I took her to the Tennessee Theater in downtown Knoxville to see one of the sappiest movies of all time, "Love Story."

I actually wanted to go to the Bijou Theater and see "Billy Jack Meets the Cheerleaders." But since it was my first date with Wanda June, I decided to take her to "Love Story" so that she would get the false impression that I was a sensitive Alan Alda kind of guy.

The date turned out to be disaster. Wanda June had already read the book, "Love Story," which, as we now know, was based on the true life story of Al and Tipper Gore. I, on the other hand, had not read the book since (1) it had not been assigned in my freshman English class, and (2) there were no Cliffs Notes available.

But since Wanda June had already read the book, she knew that Tipper or Jenny, played by the beautiful Ali McGraw, was going to croak at the end of the film, right in Al or Oliver's (played by the lovely Ryan O'Neal) arms. Consequently, Wanda June started crying at the start of the film and blubbered all through it as if she were Halle Berry accepting the Oscar.

I on the other hand, being a typical guy, watched the film impatiently, hoping to see Ali do a nude scene featuring either full frontal nudity or full nudal frontity.

The highlight of the film (at least as far as Wanda June was concerned) came just before Ali McGraw croaked. To my disappointment, a fully clothed Ali breathlessly said to Ryan O'Neal, "Love means never having to say you're sorry!"

I can't remember what Ryan O'Neal said in response. Since he was a Harvard law student, he should have said, "No, Tipper, I mean Ali, or rather, Jenny. Litigation means never having to say you're sorry. Or at least given the threat of litigation, it's not a very good idea to say you're sorry."

Those of us who are trial lawyers confront time and time again the issue of whether a post-tort apology is an admission of liability in a subsequent civil lawsuit.

The natural human instinct, particularly for us Southerners, is to apologize after an unfortunate event, even when we are not at fault. When we say we're "sorry," we don't mean we've done anything wrong. We just mean we are sorry that something bad has happened.

Unfortunately, most judges don't see it that way. Consequently, testimony that one's adversary apologized after an accident is generally admitted for consideration by the jury as an admission of fault.

During my career as a trial lawyer, I have defended many clients who, in the face of a lawsuit, have asked a very sensible question: "Can't I just apologize for what happened and move on?"

I have invariably responded, "Sure, you can apologize. But in order to move on, your verbal apology will have to be accompanied by a rectangular apology."

You know what a rectangular apology is. It's an apology that includes a dollar amount and a signature and can be deposited in a bank account.

I've been in numerous lawsuits over the years where my adversary has told me, "All my client is looking for is an apology."

However, on those occasions when I've indicated that an apology would be forthcoming, I've quickly been told the rectangular apology was also a part of the deal.

But according to a recent article in the ABA *Journal*, some jurisdictions are now reconsidering the question of whether an apology should be considered an admission of liability. At least two friendly states — Massachusetts and Georgia — have passed so-called "benevolent gesture" statutes that exclude as evidence of admission of liability in civil cases all "actions which convey a sense of compassion or commiseration emanating from human impulses."

Georgia also excludes actions "made on the impulse of benevolence or sympathy." I'm not quite sure what this means, but I think it means an impulsive "I'm sorry" statement would not come into evidence as an excited utterance admission of liability, unless the statement went something like this: "I sure am sorry I got drunk and ran my pick-up in the back of your family's minivan."

But even in states that have no "benevolent gesture statute," some law professors who never try cases are suggesting that we non-professors who do try cases should encourage our clients to apologize. These professors take the approach that if an apology does not settle the case, a jury would subsequently look kindly on our client for his or her contrition. Southern Methodist University law professor Daniel Shuman is quoted in the ABA *Journal* as saying, "We ought to encourage apology for those individuals for whom it is therapeutic, and we ought to allow juries to consider this."

Well, I'm sorry Professor Shuman, but that's precisely the problem. One litigant's therapy may be another litigant's admission by a party opponent.

I'm sorry, folks, but I'm afraid that when it comes to litigation, the great legal philosopher John Wayne was right. As he said in "Billy Jack Meets the Cheerleaders," "Never say you're sorry. It's a sign of weakness."

Having said that, I sure wish I knew where Wanda June is these days. I'd like to tell her I'm sorry I laughed all the way through "Love Story."

• • •

Will 60 Minutes Survive 60 Lawsuits?

There is an old joke that goes you know you're going to have a bad day when you arrive for work only to find the crew of "60 Minutes" waiting for you in your office lobby.

For nearly 30 years, the CBS news program "60 Minutes" has been one of the nation's highest-rated TV shows. The show is known for its hard-hitting investigative journalism. For example, during a recent episode, the notorious Al Gore withered under cross-examination by "60 Minutes" reporter Leslie Stahl and confessed that he wasn't really running for president after all.

But Morley Safer, Mike Wallace, Andy Rooney and the whole "60 Minutes" news team may have met their match in a place called Jefferson County, Miss. And when this fight is over, "60 Minutes" may soon be replaced by "60 Lawsuits."

"60 Minutes" recently broadcast a segment called "Jackpot Justice." The segment focused on two trials in the Jefferson County courthouse in which jurors awarded the plaintiffs $150 million in damages.

I didn't see the segment. It was run the same time as a re-run of the "Andy Griffith Show" was on another channel, and given a choice between Morley Safer and Barney Fife, I'm gonna watch Barney every time.

But apparently the "Jackpot Justice" episode of "60 Minutes" was seen in Jefferson County, Miss., and the folks there who saw it were not amused. In fact, what they saw made them good and mad. They got so mad, in fact, that they picked up their phones and called some of the fine trial lawyers in Jefferson County, Miss. And if you don't believe there are any fine trial lawyers in Jefferson County, Miss., well, just ask the two companies that recently got tagged for $150 million bucks a piece.

Well, those fine Mississippi trial lawyers responded by walking over to the exact spot where "60 Minutes" had filmed its "Jackpot

Justice" segment, specifically, the Jefferson County courthouse. And when they got to the courthouse, these fine Mississippi trial lawyers filed lawsuits against "60 Minutes" and CBS, claiming that the news segment slandered seven fine citizens of Jefferson County, Miss. who had previously served on the Jefferson County juries that returned the big verdicts.

And just to make sure that they got the attention of those fancy-pants Yankee lawyers who represent CBS, these fine Mississippi trial lawyers put in the complaint filed on behalf of two of the jurors that they wanted an award of $597 million in actual damages against "60 Minutes" and CBS, and $5.9 billion in punitive damages.

Oh, and by the way, they also demanded a jury to hear the case. A jury of very fine citizens from Jefferson County, mind you.

Only seven jurors have filed suit so far, but there are many other fine folks in Jefferson County who also served on the juries that were featured in the "60 Minutes" "Jackpot Justice" program. And the statute of limitations has not run on the claims of these other jurors. Consequently, "60 Minutes" may soon be meeting 60 lawsuits.

Well, I have spent some time in some Mississippi courtrooms, and I know a lot of Mississippi trial lawyers. And based on my personal experience, let me send this message to Morley and Mike and Leslie and Andy (Rooney, not Griffith) and all them other Yankees at CBS News up in New York City. You guys better take these lawsuits mighty seriously. If you don't, Trent Lott may soon replace Dan Rather as the host of the CBS Evening News.

You may laugh about those country lawyers down in Mississippi. But before you laugh too much, you might just want to call the Marlboro Man.

You remember the Marlboro Man, don't you? Why he was just about the toughest, meanest hombre in the west, riding around high in his saddle, puffing on an unfiltered cigarette.

And then the Marlboro Man came face-to-face with a Mississippi trial lawyer named Dickey Scruggs, who just so happens to be Trent Lott's brother-in-law. Unlike Trent, Dickey did not apologize to the Marlboro Man. Instead he proceeded to knock the Marlboro Man off his saddle for billions of dollars.

And if you don't believe the Marlboro Man, Mike Wallace, just call Ronald McDonald. He's been missing a lot of happy meals now that he's facing class action lawsuits claiming that he is responsible for making every child in America look like the Pillsbury Doughboy.

No, Morley, I'm afraid you're not going to be able to handle this fight in Jefferson County armed with just your camera and a microphone. You're going to have to get your own mean, tough lawyer, and I'm not talking about Alan Dershowitz. You'd better get you a Mississippi phone book, look in the yellow pages under "Attorneys," and find yourself some Mississippi trial lawyer named Bubba. Trust me on this, Leslie. If on your return trip to the Jefferson County courthouse you show up with the chair of the First Amendment Legal Defense Fund from Harvard, why you'll just end up as a little greasy spot on the Jefferson County Courthouse Square.

You see, Morley, folks in Jefferson County, Miss. don't like CBS. In fact, they haven't liked CBS since it took "Hee Haw" off the air. And if you think the next jury you see in Jefferson County will be weeping for the First Amendment during your defense lawyer's closing argument, well you've got a lot to learn.

Those smart reporters for "60 Minutes" thought they knew all about "Jackpot Justice" in Mississippi.

Heck, Bubba, they ain't seen nothing yet.

• • •

Coming Soon: My Cousin Vinny's Mediation

I went to law school for one reason. I wanted to be a trial lawyer. Not a litigator or an arbitrator or a mediator, but a trial lawyer, by Darrow! I grew up watching great trial lawyers try cases. And I never even set foot in a courtroom until I became a lawyer myself. So how did I watch great trial lawyers try cases? Simple. I grew up regularly going to a "courthouse" called the Northgate Theater in downtown Frayser, Tenn. There I sat in the "gallery," munched popcorn and Raisinettes, and watched America's greatest trial lawyers including Gregory Peck ("To Kill a Mockingbird"), Jimmy Stewart ("Anatomy of a Murder"), Spencer Tracy ("Inherit the Wind"), Henry Fonda ("Young Mr. Lincoln"), and even Woody Allen (as "Fielding Mellish" defending himself in "Bananas").

Often I didn't even have to leave the house to watch great trial lawyers in action. I would sit in the "courthouse" of my family living room in front of the black and white Philco TV and watch great trial lawyers such as Raymond Burr ("Perry Mason") or E.G. Marshall ("The Defenders").

When I was a boy, I would even watch great trial lawyers on Chistmas Eve as I would sit by the light of our family Christmas tree and watch a legendary lawyer named Fred Gayley defend Santa Claus in "Miracle on 34th Street." When the movie was over, I would always know that Santa was indeed coming to my house, thanks to the great Fred Gayley, the lawyer who saved Christmas!

Inspired by these great Hollywood trial lawyers, I dreamed of growing up to be a lawyer. I dreamed of someday standing in front of juries and reading the *Farmer's Almanac* like Henry Fonda did to prove there was no moon in the sky on the night in question.

I dreamed of conducting a cross-examination like the great Raymond Burr, wearing down both the witness on the stand and the real killer in the courtroom, so that eventually my cross-examination would be interrupted as the real killer would jump up from the gallery and yell, "Stop it, Mr. Mason! Uh, I mean, Mr. Haltom! Stop it! Your client didn't kill the victim, I did!"

And I even dreamed of defending Santa Claus in a lunacy hearing in the Shelby County Probate Court. ("This man is not crazy, Ladies and Gentlemen of the jury! He is the Real Santa Claus!")

And so I became a lawyer. I didn't become one by going to Hollywood. Instead, I went to Knoxville.

I thought that my three years of law school would be something of a film festival, as my fellow law students and I would sit in class all day and watch classic trial movies such as "Twelve Angry Men," "Witness for the Prosecution" and "The Caine Mutiny." I thought it would be a sort of Potter Stewart Film Festival. ("I can't define great trial lawyers, but I know them when I see them.") But instead I sat through three years of boring classes featuring something called the "Socratic method," which meant that my teachers didn't have to prepare for class, they just had to ask questions.

When I graduated from law school 25 years ago, I was convinced that I was about to enter the glamorous world of trial lawyering. I couldn't wait to meet my innocent clients, help them find the real killers, and save Christmas.

And then I discovered a terrible secret about the American legal system: Very few lawyers actually try cases.

Moreover, I discovered that if you get outside the city limits of Hollywood, Calif., there are very few trial lawyers. I found that the American legal profession is over-populated by an animal called a "litigator." Litigators are lawyers who claim to try cases, but they really don't. They get cases "ready for trial" by collecting documents and taking depositions. They do appear in courtrooms from time to time, but only to ask the judge to continue a trial date since the one thing a litigator never wants to do is to actually try a case.

For the past 25 years, I have tried to be a trial lawyer in a profession that increasingly regards trials as politically incorrect. And in the process, I have discovered another ironic secret about the American legal profession. These days more and more Americans are filing lawsuits, but fewer and fewer cases are ever going to trial.

If you are a skeptical litigator who doesn't believe me, just consider the evidence. According to a recent study by the American Bar Association as reported in *The New York Times*, there were five times as many lawsuits filed last year as there were forty years ago. However, in 1962, 11.5% of all civil cases filed in federal court went to trial. But now the number of cases actually going to trial in our federal court system has dropped to 1.8%.

In 1962, the average federal judge (U. S. District Judge Joe Average of Peoria) conducted 39 trials a year. But now your average federal judge (U. S. District Judge Angela Average of Boca Raton) tries only 13 cases a year.

This raises the obvious question: What do lawyers and judges outside of Hollywood do for a living? The answer apparently is litigate and mediate. That's right. We lawyers take depositions, collect reams of documents, and then spend days and nights in something called "mediations," where the lawyers and the clients all join hands, sing Kum Ba Ya, and in the words of former California litigant Rodney King, ask, "Why can't we all just get along?"

John Grisham's next best-selling novel will probably be entitled "The Runaway Mediation," soon to be a minor motion picture.

Meanwhile, there are still great trial lawyers in Hollywood. Tom Cruise is conducting cross-examinations like Perry Mason ("You can't handle the truth!") and My Cousin Vinny is still winning jury trials for his clients, "two yutes," before Alabama juries. But even in Hollywood, jury trials may soon go the way of the dinosaur or Democrats in the White House. Coming soon: "My Cousin Vinny's Alternative Dispute Resolution."

All of this makes me greatly concerned about the future of Christmas. If next December Santa Claus finds himself in an involuntary commitment proceeding in the Shelby County Probate Court, will his lawyer suggest that Christmas be mediated?

• • •

We the Jury Unanimously Find ...
That the Law is Really Stupid!

J urors are mighty powerful people. If you don't believe me, just ask O.J. Simpson. Thanks to a jury, O.J. is a free man who spends every day of his life looking for the "real killers." Apparently, he thinks they are hiding out on a golf course.

Yep, no doubt about it, juries are mighty powerful. In fact, they may be the only thing doctors fear.

Juries can send the guilty to death row, free the innocent, tend to the sick and wounded, or redistribute the wealth.

Like Robin Hood, jurors can take from the rich and give to the poor, although when they do, generally the poor man's lawyer takes a third of the money that's being redistributed from the rich.

As a buddy of mine who practices in Weakley County once said, "Juries are more powerful than Tarzan's armpits!"

But hold on to the keys to your Lexus, doctor! As powerful as juries already are, they may soon become even more powerful!

On November 5, voters in South Dakota will decide on a proposed constitutional amendment that would allow juries to refuse to follow any law that they believe is unfair, unwise or misguided. It's a concept known as "jury nullification," and it basically empowers a jury to pretty much do what they want to do. For example, a jury could find a defendant guilty of a crime but could nevertheless let him go free because they think that what he did shouldn't have been against the law in the first place.

Similar jury nullification amendments have been proposed in other states as well.

Empowered by "jury nullification," jurors could properly accept what criminal defense lawyers have long called the "he had it coming to him defense." This is a defense that is not taught in any law school, but it basically goes like this: "Ladies and gentlemen of the jury, my client, Bubba here, is accused of murdering Joe Bob. And you know what? Bubba did it! That's right, he killed Joe Bob! And you and I and everybody here in Hootersville know why Bubba did it! He did it because Joe Bob was a low-down, ornery, no-count, worthless piece of trailer park trash, who was always mean to Bubba and to you and to me and to everybody else in this town, so ole Joe Bob had it coming to him!" (JURY RESPONDS WITH CHEERS AND SEVERAL JURORS TRY TO START THE "WAVE.")

Up until now, we lawyers have had to be somewhat subtle in advancing the he-had-it-coming-to-him-defense, just as we have had to be subtle in arguing the this-is-a-really-stupid-law-so-you-should-ignore-it defense. But in the brave new world of jury nullification, we can tell the jury, "Hey, folks, don't worry about what the judge tells you! Make your own law and apply it!"

Legal experts across the country are appalled by the proposed jury nullification amendment because they see it as taking away one teeny-tiny little restraint that, at least theoretically, has always been placed on a jury. That restraint is called "the law." Why even in old Judge Roy Bean's courtroom, jurors have always been told that they must follow the law and give the defendant a fair trial before they hang him!

These legal experts contend that there is a thin line between a jury and a lynch mob, and if jury nullification becomes the law (or, more accurately, the anti-law), jury trials may start to resemble "The Jerry Springer Show" or "talk radio listeners' day" at the Tennessee legislature.

Well, I'm no Nina Totenberg, and you won't be seeing me on an upcoming edition of "Court TV." Nevertheless, I think all the concern about "jury nullification" is just much legal ado about nothing.

Jurors have always been the 800-pound gorilla of the American legal system. They sleep where they want to sleep (often in the jury box during a trial) and they do what they want to do. They follow the law when it is convenient, and ignore it when it gets in the way of their pursuit of justice (just like U.S. Supreme Court justices!). And in the process, they generally manage to reach the right result. This point is perhaps best illustrated by a story the great Don Paine tells about a jury trial that was held a few years ago in a small town in the mountains of East Tennessee.

The defendant was charged with stealing a mule. As the prosecutor put on his case, two things quickly became (in the words of a former lawyer-president) perfectly clear to the jury and everyone else in the courtroom. First, the evidence was overwhelming that the defendant had in fact stolen the mule. But second, it was also clear that the poor defendant desperately needed a mule to help him plow his small plot of land and feed his family.

After both the prosecution and defense had rested, the judge read the law to the jury and then sent them to the jury room to deliberate. After just a few minutes, the jury returned.

"Ladies and gentlemen of the jury, have you reached a verdict?" asked the Judge.

"Yes we have," replied the jury foreperson. "We find the defendant not guilty, but he's got to give back the mule!"

The wise Judge said, "Ladies and gentlemen of the jury, I cannot accept your verdict. It is what the law calls an 'inconsistent verdict.' You cannot find the defendant not guilty but say that he has to give back that which you have told me he did not steal. Accordingly, I am going to send you back to the jury room to resume your deliberations."

The jury retired again to the jury room, but returned about five minutes later.

"Have you now reached a new verdict?" asked the judge.

"Yes we have, your Honor," replied the foreperson. "We find the defendant not guilty . . . and he can keep the mule!"

• • •

An Exciting New Era for CPAs

Some of my best friends are CPAs, although I wouldn't want my daughter to marry one.

For generations, CPAs have had a well-deserved image of being about as exciting as Dick Cheney. The dull and boring image of America's CPAs is probably best illustrated by the following joke that was told to me by a CPA:

Question: Do you know an actuary is?

Answer: He's someone who does not have the personality to be a certified public accountant.

Not very funny? Of course not. Remember, the joke was told to me by a CPA, and "funny CPA" is an oxymoron, like jumbo shrimp or working vacation or student athlete.

For years, CPAs have tried in vain to change their button-down image. A few years ago the American Institute of Certified Public Accountants hired a Boston advertising agency to produce TV and radio commercials designed to convince the American people that CPAs are really a bunch of fun-loving men and women whose idea of a good time does not involve spreadsheets and IRS Form 1040As. The TV commercials featured young, hip CPAs screaming, "Whassup?!"

For the life of me, I cannot figure out why the American Institute of Certified Public Accountants wanted to change the image of America's CPA. I for one want my CPA to be a boring guy. I want him to look just like Ward Cleaver. I want him to listen to old Lawrence Welk records while he prepares my tax returns or financial statements for my office.

Who wants a wild and crazy CPA, anyway? Do you really want your tax return prepared by some guy who wears an earring and sports a tattoo that reads, "Born to Audit!"?

Do we really want your 401k managed by some gal wearing blue jeans and a tank top that reads, "CPAs Never Lose their Balance!"?

But here's some good news for CPAs who want to shed their Bob Newhart image. Thanks to the Enron scandal, America's CPAs may soon enter an exciting new era. Indeed, the Enron scandal may be for CPAs what the Watergate scandal was for us lawyers.

Prior to the Watergate scandal nearly 30 years ago, we lawyers were highly respected. Consequently, we were also boring.

You didn't see many lawyers on TV or in movies prior to Watergate. And the few Hollywood lawyers you did see in those days were honorable and respected men like Perry Mason, Hamilton Burger or Atticus Finch.

But then came Watergate, an era when the attorney general of the United States led a procession of lawyers to prison, not as a prosecutor, but as a fellow inmate! Suddenly we lawyers were no longer respected and boring. We became bad guys, and consequently, we also became the source of endless fascination by the American public.

In the post-Watergate era, the legal profession has taken over every aspect of American life, even entertainment. Indeed, lawyers have become Hollywood's biggest stars.

It's been move over, Perry Mason! Make way for Ally McBeal!. Good-bye, Earl Warren! Hello, Judge Judy!

In the post-Watergate era, we lawyers have even taken over America's book stores. As you read these words, millions of Americans are flocking to Books 'R' Us to buy a copy of John Grisham's latest legal thriller.

But now that one of America's biggest CPA firms, Arthur Andersen, has become involved in the Enron scandal, accountants may soon join lawyers on the public's list of bad guys. And take it from me, this will be the greatest thing ever to happen to CPAs.

In the post-Enron era, Hollywood will soon produce movies and

TV shows about ruthless, sexy accountants. In fact, NBC is already working on its new prime-time series, "L.A. Accounting." It will be the compelling story of vicious CPAs who recklessly audit their clients and then make love to them.

John Grisham is reportedly working on a new novel, "The Runaway Audit," the story of Chatsworth Harrington III, a young Houston CPA who fearlessly shreds millions of client financial records in the face of a congressional investigation.

And finally, Julia Roberts is already cast in the lead role in the upcoming blockbuster motion picture, "Pretty CPA," co-starring Jon Voight as Arthur Andersen.

• • •

Is a Sleeping Lawyer Still on the Job?

Benjamin Franklin once wrote, "Early to bed and early to rise makes a man healthy, wealthy, and not a whole lot of fun." Well, if this is true, none of us are going to get the flu this winter, and America is not about to enter a recession. Why? Simple. It's nap time in America!

According to several published news reports, our healthy, wealthy and boring president, George Dubya Bush, goes to bed at 9:30 every night. He'll probably give his next State of the Union Address while wearing footie pajamas and clutching his teddy bear, Chad.

President Dubya's early bedtime is something that hasn't been seen at the White House since the Reagan administration. In fact, if they ever make a movie about President Dubya's years in the White House, it will probably be called, "Bedtime for Bonzo — The Sequel."

President Dubya is apparently not the only sleepy American who is turning in early these days. According to a recent article in The New York Times (the early edition, I might add), increasingly more and more Americans are going to bed long before David Letterman's monologue. The night owl Clinton years are over. We Americans are pooped and ready to catch some serious Z's.

More and more Americans are also taking naps. This could actually be bad news for the American economy because most of these naps do not take place on either Saturday or Sunday afternoon. No, many Americans are reportedly catching their 40 winks right on the job site by dozing off at their desks or nodding off during boring "bidness meetings."

And I don't mean to disturb your daily nap, but here is some real disturbing news. Are you ready? I don't want to sound an alarm, but wake up and listen. Some of those Americans who are reportedly sleeping on the job these days are ... I hate to say it, but it's true ...

yes, lawyers.

Yes, my fellow lawyers, it's no dream. Some of us are actually sleeping on the job these days. We are falling asleep during depositions and conference calls, and a few of us are even joining the judge and jury in sleeping through trials.

Make no mistake about it, it's a legal nightmare. If you don't believe me, consider this: Napping on the job has become so prevalent that the United States Court of Appeals for the Fifth Circuit is now struggling with an intriguing legal question: Is a sleeping lawyer still on the job? More specifically, can a snoring defense lawyer effectively represent a client at trial?

This legal issue has been raised on behalf of a Texas criminal defendant who claims that his court-appointed lawyer slept through most of his trial, only waking up when a wide-awake jury screamed out the verdict, "Guilty!" (That probably woke up Rip Van Lawyer.)

A panel of judges from the Fifth Circuit recently heard arguments in the case, although some of the judges reportedly nodded off during the proceedings. One of the judges actually missed the oral argument because he overslept.

A decision is expected in the next few weeks. For the time being, the judges are just sleeping on the matter.

This could be a very dangerous case and could make for some sleepless nights in the history of American jurisprudence. Suppose the federal appeals court decides to let sleeping lawyers lie and rules that a lawyer who sleeps during trial is still on the job.

Or they could rule that it is just a case of harmless error since the bed was on fire when the lawyer got in it. If this happens, why the next thing you know airline pilots will claim they can sleep in the cockpit. Surgeons will claim a constitutional right to snore during operations. Preachers will claim they can sleep through their sermons, just like the rest of us. And President Dubya may sleep through the next cabinet meeting, a not unprecedented doze in American presidential history.

No doubt about it, it's time for America's lawyers to wake up, smell the coffee, and tackle these challenging sleep-related legal issues.

Now if you will excuse me (yawn), I'm going to take a nap.

• • •

PART VII:
BUT SERIOUSLY, FOLKS

Good-Bye, Atticus

When I was a little boy, I had lots of heroes. Most of them were either cowboys or baseball players. Among my cowboy heroes were Roy Rogers, the Lone Ranger and Hop-Along Cassidy. My baseball heroes included Mickey Mantle, Willie Mays and Bob Gibson.

But I had two heroes that to my knowledge never rode a horse or shot an outlaw. And instead of carrying bats, they toted briefcases.

Believe it or not, these two heroes were lawyers.

They weren't real lawyers, mind you. When I was a boy, I didn't know any real lawyers. My daddy was a preacher, not a lawyer, and there were no lawyers in our neighborhood. As best I could recall, there wasn't a single lawyer in the whole community of Frayser, Tenn.

But the two fictional lawyers who became my heroes were very real to me during my childhood, and remain heroes for me to this day.

The first heroic lawyer in my life was Perry Mason. Perry was a phenomenal lawyer who had two incredible attributes. First, he always represented innocent people. Second, he always won.

A few years after I met Perry, I met another heroic lawyer, who appeared not on my TV screen but on the big screen at the Northgate Theatre in downtown Frayser.

I was 12 years old, and I sat in the Northgate Theatre and watched a "picture show" that did more than entertain me. It moved me. It challenged me. It inspired me. And I've never gotten over it.

The picture show was called "To Kill a Mockingbird," and it was the compelling story of Atticus Finch, a country lawyer from Maycomb, Ala.

Unlike Perry Mason, Atticus was not a rich, successful lawyer. He was a poor, struggling one.

Atticus did have one thing in common with Perry Mason. He represented an innocent client, Tom Robinson.

But unlike Perry, Atticus lost. Tom Robinson, an innocent man, was convicted by a racist jury.

Justice always prevailed on Perry Mason, but it didn't in "To Kill a Mockingbird."

I will never forget the climactic scene of the film. After losing the biggest case of his career, Atticus packs his brief case and slowly walks out of the courtroom. As he is departing, the courthouse gallery, packed with the African-American citizens of Maycomb, spontaneously rises in his honor. Sitting in the front row of the gallery, along side Tom Robinson's preacher, Reverend Sykes, are Atticus' children, Scout and Jim. Reverend Sykes leans over to Scout, calls her by her formal name, and whispers, "Miss Jean Louise, stand up. Your father is passing."

That scene changed my life. It made me forget all about cowboys and baseball players. It made me want to grow up to be a lawyer. Not a "successful" lawyer like Perry, but a courageous one like Atticus.

A few days ago, I heard the news that Atticus had died. The news came not from Maycomb, Ala., but from Hollywood. Gregory Peck, the wonderful actor who portrayed Atticus, had passed away at the age of 87.

When I heard the news, I recalled the wonderful moment nearly 40 years ago when I sat in the Northgate Theatre and watched Atticus Finch lose a trial, pack his briefcase and slowly walk out of an Alabama courtroom.

It is an image that I will carry with me for the rest of my life. Atticus departed the Maycomb courthouse that day personifying victory, not defeat. And he inspired me in a way that a Perry Mason cross-examination or a Mickey Mantle home run never could.

So good-bye, Atticus. If I ever grow up, I hope to be just like you.

• • •

Remembering Judge Wyeth Chandler

My hometown of Memphis recently lost one of its icons, Judge Wyeth Chandler. I first met Judge Chandler in 1982 when he became a circuit court judge. I had followed his public career since my high school days in the late 1960s when he was first elected to the Memphis City Council. When he was elected mayor in 1971, I was off at college, but I read about him most every day when a copy of *The Commercial Appeal* arrived by mail to my dorm, a couple of days after publication. This was in the days before Al Gore invented the Internet.

Will Rogers once said, "All I know is what I read in the papers." I was the same way about then-Mayor Chandler. I read about his late night escapades ("The Mayor needs help!"), his conflicts with police and firemen, and his impromptu concerts at Hernando's Hideaway where he would croon, "Give me Memphis, Tennessee!" Based on what I read, I concluded as a college student that Judge Chandler was arrogant, condescending, and something of a caricature, like Foghorn Leghorn in the old Bugs Bunny cartoons ("I say, that's a joke, son!").

And then one day in 1982 I met Judge Chandler at the courthouse. Within minutes after receiving his warm handshake, I realized that every pre-conceived notion I had about the man was absolutely wrong.

Arrogant? Just the opposite. He was warm, down-to-earth, and possessed a wonderful self-deprecating sense of humor.

Condescending? No way. He was a powerful man for one simple reason. He transferred importance and power to others. Whether he was meeting with Federal Express CEO Fred Smith or a janitor at City Hall or a then-young lawyer like myself, he treated everyone the same. He'd rivet you with eye contact, ask you a million questions about yourself and your family and your background, and make you feel like the most important person in the world.

I was a lawyer in the first jury trial Judge Chandler conducted after Governor Lamar Alexander appointed him to the bench. He started the proceedings by doing something that was quintessentially Wyeth Chandler. Before a jury panel was brought into the courtroom, Judge Chandler addressed the lawyers and said, "Now I have to tell you something. I'm a brand spanking new judge and I don't know what I'm doing. The last time I tried a case as a lawyer Lyndon Johnson was president, so I'm counting on you guys to help me out." That was vintage Wyeth Chandler. He was a leader not because he did things for people, but because he asked people to do things for him and for themselves.

In the years that followed that first jury trial, I got to know Judge Chandler as a dear friend. I also got to know his dog, Millie. Judge Chandler is the only judge I've ever known who would bring his dog into the courtroom. During non-jury trials, Judge Wyeth and "Judge Millie" would both preside. Judge Chandler would sit at the bench with Millie on his lap. He would pet her while dispensing justice, and would sometimes call for a recess so that, in the Judge's words, "Millie can take care of her bidness."

Judge Chandler never had an unexpressed thought. If something popped in his mind, it would come rolling out of his mouth. He was totally undiplomatic. If he'd been Secretary of State, World War III would have happened a long time ago. But his candor made him a wonderful judge, and although I didn't know him in the 1970s, I suspect it made him a fine mayor. Even if you disagreed with the man, you just couldn't get mad at him. He would say outrageous things, laugh at himself, and just win you over.

After retiring from the bench several years ago, the judge spent the last few years of his life as a mediator, trying to help people resolve conflicts without going to court. He was the best mediator I ever saw. He knew how to bring people together. On many occasions, I saw him sit down with folks who had lost a child or a spouse in an accident. He would hold their hands, cry with them, console them, and then tell them it was time to resolve the conflict and move on with life. Judge Chandler was good at this because he practiced what he preached. He lived life passionately both in times of laughter and times of tears.

One morning last spring I got a phone call from Judge Chandler's secretary. She said the judge wanted me to know that his beloved Millie had passed away. I called the judge's house and left a message of condolence on his answering machine. And then I left my office, walked three blocks to the Shelby County Courthouse, and spent a few moments in the courtroom of Division 1, remembering the days when Millie and Judge Wyeth presided.

I'll be back in that courtroom soon to try a case or argue a motion before Judge Chandler's successor, Judge John McCarroll. He's a fine judge, although he doesn't bring his dog to court, and he often gives himself the luxury of an unexpressed thought. There was, after all, only one Wyeth Chandler.

• • •

Remembering My Buddy Tom

On April 21, 2004, my buddy and brother lawyer Tom Parrish passed away after a valiant battle with cancer. He was 46. Tom was Elizabeth's daddy, Gwen's husband, Jim and Julie's brother, and a dear friend to all of us who were blessed to share a life with him.

Tom and I were friends were over 20 years. For the first 15 years of that friendship, Tom was my buddy. For the last five, as he fought and whipped cancer time and time again, he was my minister. Not an ordained clergyman, mind you, but a minister in the true meaning of the word. His life was a daily sermon about love and faith and grace.

The great American philosopher Mae West once said, "You only go around once in life, but if you play your cards right, once is enough."

Tom always played his cards right, even when he was dealt a lousy hand.

I first met Tom back in the 1980s. He was your typical up and coming young lawyer in a hurry. Tom had both a law degree and an MBA, and he possessed the most important skill you can find in a lawyer. He knew how to make things happen. He was constantly in demand by bankers and "bidnessmen" who sought to launch new enterprises. And Tom helped them do it.

During the go-go '80s, Tom was constantly in motion. He rushed through life as if he were a Titans quarterback executing the two minute drill.

Tom did it all. He negotiated deals, became the lay leader of his church, led civic groups, and served as president of his college's alumni association. He could have been the official poster child for the National Decaffeinated Coffee Council.

As the '80s gave way to the '90s, Tom devoted himself to the most important work of his life. He and his wife adopted a beautiful baby girl named Elizabeth, and not surprisingly, Tom became the greatest dad since Ward Cleaver.

Tom had it all. The wonderful wife, the beautiful intelligent daughter, devoted friends, a rewarding law career, leadership positions in his church and his community.

And then, on a spring day nearly five years ago, Tom found out that he had cancer. Not just ordinary cancer, mind you, if there is such a thing. But a very rare cancer that in Tom's words, both intrigued and baffled doctors.

And then a miracle happened. In the face of death, this wonderful young man began living life more fully than ever. He took an extended leave from his law practice and devoted each day to his faith, his family and his friends.

A couple of years ago, during a brief wonderful interlude when Tom's cancer was in remission, he gathered family and friends in his church for a special thanksgiving service. Tom was the preacher that day, and I will never forget his words. Tom told the congregation, "I'm not glad I have cancer, and I wish it would just go away. But I'm glad for what it's done. I'm grateful for the miracles it has brought to my life and for the awareness of love from each of you and the love from God that surrounds me each second of the day."

Well, I seriously doubt they have the *Tennessee Bar Journal* in Heaven. But Tom, if you're reading this, here's a message: Thanks, buddy. Thanks for all the love and the laughter and the joy. Thanks for trying to teach me how to suffer with grace and live each day with faith and hope. Thanks, Tom, for being the most alive person I ever knew.

• • •

Mommas, Let Your Babies Grow Up to be Lawyers

For my 12th birthday, my mother gave me a Bible. Not just any Bible, mind you, but a *Scofield Reference Bible*, just like the one my father (Reverend Bill Haltom Sr.) preached from in the pulpit each Sunday morning. The Bible had a beautiful leather cover with my name inscribed in gold letters at the front on the bottom right-hand corner.

The *Scofield Reference Bible* was in the King James version, of course. We Haltoms were Southern fried Baptists, and we fervently believed that among the many miracles in the New Testament was the fact that Jesus spoke in Elizabethan English some 1500 years before Shakespeare and King James were even around. As my grandmother used to say, "If the King James version of the Bible was good enough for Paul and Silas, it's good enough for me!" She might have added, it's also good enough for thee.

My mother's gift came with a mighty big string attached. Mom said, "I know you will use this Bible for the rest of your life because I believe the Lord is calling you to be a preacher like your father."

My heart sank. I wasn't sure the Lord was calling me to the ministry, but Momma definitely was. I had a terrible confession to make. "Mom," I said, "I don't want to be a preacher. I want to be a lawyer."

My mother did not conceal her disappointment. "Your father and I have raised you to be a Christian," she said. "I'm not sure you can be a Christian and a lawyer."

Some 40 years later, the Bible Mom gave me for my 12th birthday now sits on the credenza in my law office, right next to my copy of *Black's Law Dictionary*. Mom is in heaven now. She passed away in 1966, just a couple of years after admonishing me to use my Bible to pursue grace, not law.

I think about my mom every day, and I can't help but wonder if she would be disappointed that the Bible she gave me is now found in a law office rather than a pastor's study. And I also struggle with whether Mom was right to doubt that one could be a person of faith and also a lawyer.

After 27 years of law practice, I've decided that my wonderful mother may not have had the right answer, but she definitely raised the right question. I believe that Mom was right that each of us are called to the ministry. Some folks are called to the ordained ministry. Others of us are called to a life of ministry as doctors, teachers, artists, architects, auto mechanics, and yes, lawyers.

I sincerely believe that a life in the law can be a life of ministry. I also believe that a life of a lawyer is not just about law. It's also about grace and forgiveness and understanding.

As a trial lawyer, I have a chance every day to minister to my clients and to receive their ministry in return. It is both an awesome responsibility and a wonderful blessing to be an advocate for a brother or sister in conflict. At our worst moments, we lawyers can create or sustain conflict. But when we do our job right — when we minister — we resolve conflicts, heal divisions and restore just relationships.

The Bible Mom gave me has a slender blue ribbon attached to the binding. The ribbon serves as a bookmark, and I always keep it at my favorite passage. It is the words of the prophet Micah: "What doth the Lord require of us but to do mercy, to love justice, and to walk humbly with our God."

I read that passage from time to time as I sit in my law office. And when I do, I remember my mother and hope that in my daily work, I will in some small way answer her call to a life of ministry.

• • •

ABOUT THE AUTHOR

Bill Haltom is a trial lawyer (not a litigator) with the firm of Thomason, Hendrix, Harvey, Johnson and Mitchell in Memphis. He is the 2005-2006 president of the Tennessee Bar Association, a past president of the Memphis Bar Association, and a past chair of the board of editors of the ABA *Journal* and a past chair of the editorial board of the *Tennessee Bar Journal*

Bill is the author of two non-best-sellers, *Daddies: An Endangered Species* and *In Search of Hamilton Burger: The Trial and Tribulations of a Southern Lawyer.* Bill is a humor columnist for numerous publications including *The Memphis Commercial Appeal*, the *Brunswick (Georgia) News*, the *Tennessee Bar Journal*, and the Tennessee Bar Website, TBAL*ink*, at www.tba.org.

He is married to Claudia Swafford Haltom, a Juvenile Court Referee Judge in Memphis. Bill and Claudia have three children. Their real names are Will, Ken, and Margaret Grace. However, in Bill's columns he identifies them as Wally, Beaver and Her Royal Highness the Princess.

ABOUT THE ILLUSTRATOR

David Jendras (shown here with future cartoonist-grandson, Nathan) is the director of publications and new media for the ABA *Journal* and has served as president of the Society of National Association of Publications.

Dave and his wife, Gerry, have three kids (a CPA, a veterinarian and a 7th grade science teacher), one grandson and one grandaughter. Dave also did the illustrations for *In Search of Hamilton Burger: The Trial and Tribulations of a Southern Lawyer.* As Bill puts it, "Not many people liked my columns in the book, but everyone loved Dave's illustrations."